PARIS
and its Greatest Monuments in 3D

SUZANNE DE VILLARS

Notre-Dame de Paris
21

Sainte-Chapelle
27

Palais de Justice
and the Conciergerie
28

Pont Neuf and
Place Dauphine
30

Île-Saint-Louis
32

The Quays of the Seine
33

Place des Vosges
36

Hôtel de Sully
37

Musée Carnavalet
38

Musée National Picasso-Paris
42

Centre Pompidou
44

Hôtel de Soubise
46

Hôtel de Sens
47

Saint-Paul-Saint-Louis church
48

Hôtel de Ville
49

Place du Châtelet
50

Place des Victoires
51

Palais du Louvre
52

Musée du Louvre
54

Palais-Royal
58

The Jardin des Tuileries
60

Place Vendôme
63

Place de la Concorde
64

The Grand and the Petit Palais
66

Eiffel Tower
69

Champ-de-Mars
70

Hôtel des Invalides
72

Musée d'Orsay
75

Musée Rodin
78

École des Beaux-Arts
79

Institut de France
80

Pont des Arts
81

Saint-Germain-des-Prés
82

Many thanks to François Jaskarzec
for his brilliant idea.

© 2016 Parigramme / Compagnie parisienne du livre (Paris)
www.parigramme.com

Saint-Sulpice
84

Notre-Dame-du-Val-de-Grâce
85

The Palais and the Jardin du Luxembourg
86

Montparnasse
88

The Catacombs
90

The Panthéon
93

La Sorbonne
94

Hôtel de Cluny
95

Arènes de Lutèce
96

Institut du Monde Arabe
99

The Jardin des Plantes and the Grande Galerie de l'Évolution
100

Place de la Bastille
102

Canal Saint-Martin
104

Parc de La Villette and Cité des Sciences et de l'Industrie
106

Père-Lachaise cemetery
109

Montmartre
110

Musée de Montmartre
111

Sacré-Cœur
112

Opéra-Garnier
114

The Grands Boulevards
117

The Covered Passages
118

Musée Jacquemart-André
120

Musée Gustave-Moreau
121

Musée de la Vie Romantique
121

Parc Monceau
122

The Champs-Élysées
124

Arc de Triomphe
125

La Défense
128

Palais de Tokyo and the Musée d'Art Moderne
130

Palais de Chaillot
131

Musée Marmottan-Monet
132

The Bois de Boulogne
133

Fondation Louis-Vuitton
133

Château de Versailles
134

The Panthéon.

Without its great monuments, would Paris still be Paris? Not really, since they are inseparable from the city's history; the history they are the result of, the witnesses to, and, on occasion, the victims of. The siting of the city's buildings is not haphazard: the oldest, including Notre-Dame and the Sainte-Chapelle, are found on the Île-de-la-Cité—the birthplace of Paris—or nearby. The most prestigious are on the banks of the Seine, which in the classical age was no longer considered simply utilitarian, but an ornamental pond. Others, including some of the most spectacular, such as the Palais Garnier, are part of Haussmann's redesign of Paris into "the most beautiful city in the world," and are found in the privileged neighborhoods of the Second Empire. The most recent, such as the Institut du Monde Arabe, the Cité des Sciences and the Fondation Louis Vuitton, have taken form on former industrial sites.

Everything, then, is born of a particular context, at a time that defines it, and that it exceeds. The life of a monument does not stop when it appears: thus during the Revolution, palaces and places of worship were transformed into prisons; the Eiffel Tower transmitted telegraphs during the First World War; and the bells of Notre-Dame hailed the Liberation of Paris on August 26, 1944. It is sometimes even history itself that shifts a building into the ranks of "great monuments," although it was not their initial destiny: for example, the Orsay train station transformed into a museum or the abattoirs of La Villette recast as the Cité des Sciences. Sometimes it is the opposite, when human convictions tear down the stones: thus, the Revolution ruined the facade of Notre-Dame, the insurgents of the Commune burnt the Tuileries palace and dismantled the Vendôme column.

The often-invoked adage of Paris as a "city-museum" is incorrect, for it implies that life is absent. This curious expression, which seems to equate a museum with a cemetery when we would rather taste vitality, hardly applies to a capital whose monument-symbols carry all the marks of their history. The idea of the city-museum holds even less resonance as we enjoy discovering, or rediscovering, one or other building and its story, and as this becomes part of our life. Then, further increasing our *joie de vivre*, we "live" Paris.

The arrow of Notre-Dame. View on the east of Paris.

The façade of Notre-Dame de Paris.

The Pont des Arts and the Institut de France.

The Louvre's pyramid, in the Cour Napoléon.

The big nave of the Musée d'Orsay.

The Invalides, the Church of the Dôme.

The Opéra-Garnier.

The Arc de Triomphe.

The Centre Pompidou.

The July Column, Place de la Bastille.

The Sacré-Cœur Basilica.

The Eiffel Tower.

The Géode cinema and the Cité des Sciences et de l'Industrie.

The Château de Versailles.

View of the cathedral's apse.

Notre-Dame de Paris

PARVIS NOTRE-DAME, PLACE JEAN-PAUL-II (4ᵗʰ)

The summit of the south transept.

Work on Notre-Dame began in 1163, at the initiative of the bishop of Paris, Maurice de Sully. The new building was to replace the cathedral dedicated to Saint Stephen with a place of worship more in keeping with Paris, the capital of the kingdom. The work lasted more than one hundred and seventy years, without adding to the tally the reworkings that followed, those that brought the cathedral into line with the taste of the day or the desires of the rulers. In the early eighteenth century, the fulfillment of Louis XIII's vow, in thanks to the Virgin for having given him an heir, proved fatal to the medieval choir screen.

Decorated with fleurs-de-lys, as noted by Jules Michelet, Notre-Dame de Paris belongs as much to history as to religion; in the longitudinal bands cutting across the facade, the historian saw "the lines of a book, and narrate instead of praying. Notre-Dame de Paris is the church of the monarchy itself." The revolutionaries of 1793 were only partly mistaken when they attacked the Gallery of the Kings, thinking the Judean rulers represented there were the kings of France: they were cutting down the symbol. The large rose window in the south representing the heavenly court surrounding God remained in place; though much altered it has nevertheless retained fragments of its first stained glass. Mutilated, Notre-Dame was transformed into a temple of Reason under the Revolution, then it housed a warehouse for various goods, and finally it was abandoned until the early nineteenth century when it returned to being a place of worship. The architects Jean-Baptiste Lassus and Eugène Viollet-le-Duc undertook the old cathedral's rehabilitation, sometimes cutting away from the original, adding chimeras and statues according to their fancy! Another major change was the siting of a large square in front of the cathedral by the prefect Haussmann under the Second Empire, which disturbed the visual discovery of Notre-Dame. When the cathedral was still in its medieval setting, it could not be seen until turning the corner of a narrow street, thus making it more spectacular and immense in contrast with the ordinary buildings lying at its feet.

Detail of the Tree of Jesse stained-glass window.

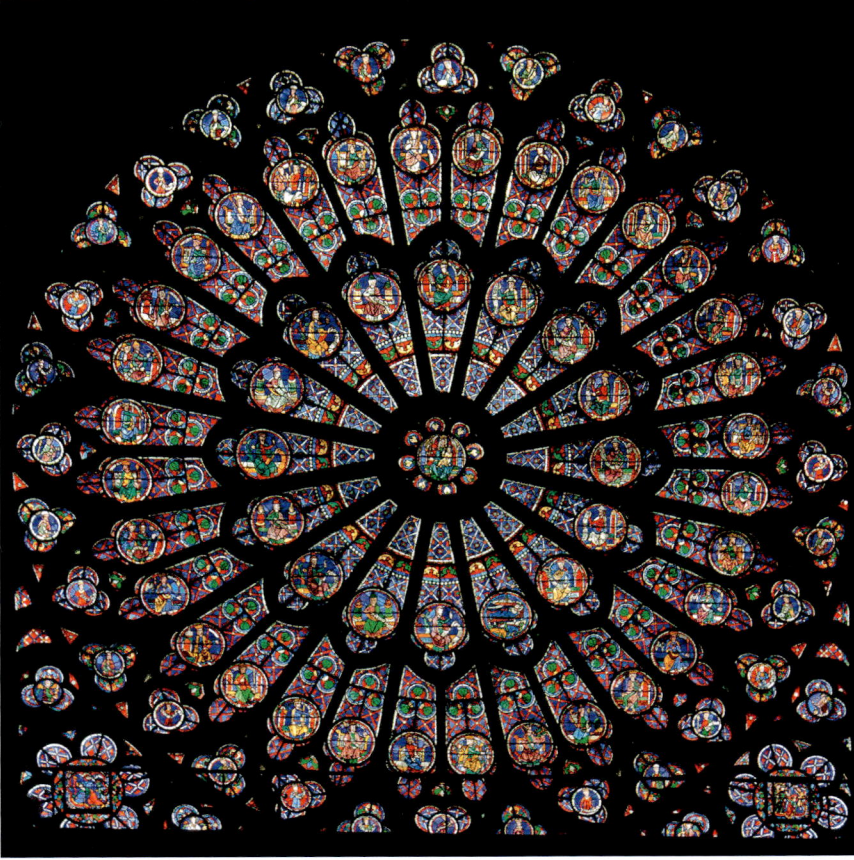
South facade rose window.

Watchful chimera.

The ambulatory, the gallery surrounding the choir, tells the life and Passion of Christ.

Statue

In his restoration work, Viollet-le-Duc endeavored to give faces back to the gallery's decapitated heads. But which faces to give them? Three of the visages weren't left to the sculptor's inspiration, but explicitly represent the architect, his associate Lassus and the inspector of works at Notre-Dame. Viollet-le-Duc is also present at the foot of the arrow, in the form of Saint Thomas.

The main facade of the Gallery of the Kings.

The great bell of the south tower.

Detail of the Portal of the Virgin.

The gilded bust of Saint Ursula (left, 15th century), the reliquary of the nail and wood of the cross (opposite) and the reliquary of the Crown of Thorns (right page, 1862) are the major pieces in Notre-Dame's Treasury.

Treasury

Pillaged during the Revolution, the Treasury was exceptionally rich. It was only partially restored, but inherited the Sainte-Chapelle's priceless relics: Christ's Crown of Thorns, a piece of the cross and a nail. The first Friday of each month, the relics of the Passion are shown to the faithful.

Under this rock ...

Under the square, excavations have revealed the substantial remains of a medieval or even Gallo-Roman city, including fragments of the city wall. A visitor to the archeological crypt need move little more than 100 meters to cross fifteen centuries of history!

A reliquary for the holy crown.

Statue of Saint Louis.

The Sainte-Chapelle and its restored spire within the confines of the Palais de Justice.

Sainte-Chapelle

8 BOULEVARD DU PALAIS (1st)

Saint Louis built the Sainte-Chapelle in his palace to house the relics of the Passion, which he bought from the emperor of Constantinople: the Crown of Thorns, a piece of the cross, a section of the lance used on the side of Jesus during his crucifixion, the sponge stained with holy blood. Consecrated in 1248, the building's narrowness is striking. It consists of two superimposed vaults; the lower chapel was accessible to all palace staff, while the upper chapel was reserved for the royal family and housed the shrine itself.

All in stained glass rather than stone, the royal chapel is itself shaped like a shrine. The Sainte-Chapelle's remarkable stained glass covers some six hundred square meters and dates from the last two thirds of the king's reign, with the notable exception of the rose window.

The building was both religious and political, located as it was within the grounds of the Palais-Royal, explicitly highlighting the link between the king and God. The king offered his people the opportunity to gather around the relics of the saints, in the same place that he took Communion.

The Revolution destroyed the Sainte-Chapelle's exterior decorations, the fleurs-de-lys and dispersed the relics.

Those that could be found were added to the Notre-Dame Treasury in the early nineteenth century. The building itself, which was transformed into an archive for the Palais de Justice, was the subject of a major restoration campaign between 1837 and 1863, during which the spire was restored.

Stained glass representing the disciples of Emmaus.

Palais de Justice and the Conciergerie
BOULEVARD DU PALAIS (1st)

This site was home to the Gallo-Roman governer's palace and then, from the High Middle Ages until the second half of the fourteenth century, to that of the kings of France. Looting by rioters—led by Étienne Marcel, provost of the merchants—was incited when Charles V moved their residences to the Hôtel Saint-Pol and the Louvre. After the sovereign's departure, the site was taken over by the administrative services of the kingdom, then its courts and bodies responsible for judicial functions.

Ravaged by several fires in the seventeenth and eighteenth centuries, the Palais de Justice was redesigned, rebuilt and expanded. Little remains of the Palais de la Cité: apart from the Sainte-Chapelle, the Conciergerie is the most significant vestige, even if its buildings were very freely restored in the nineteenth century. This prison takes its name from the "concierge," the person who kept the palace in the king's absence, keeper of the lower- and middle-ranking powers in the palace's jurisdiction. Following the king's departure in 1370, the Conciergerie's prison was extended to occupy virtually the entire lower level of the palace. François Ravaillac, the murderer of Henri IV, and Louis Dominique Cartouche, the popular bandit, were among the Ancien Régime's famous prisoners. In turn, the Revolution filled the jails of the Conciergerie, including holding Marie-Antoinette for the two and half months before her execution, and then devouring its own children. Georges Danton and Maximilien Robespierre stayed in the dark dungeons before going to the guillotine.

The Clock Tower
The clock tower, at the corner of the Boulevard du Palais and the Quai de l'Horloge, is home to the oldest public clock in Paris, put in place in 1370. A new dial, sculpted by Germain Pilon, appeared in 1585, and it is still the one we admire today.

The Conciergerie on the Quai de l'Horloge.

The dungeon of Marie-Antoinette.

Tour Bonbec

Reworked in the nineteenth century, elevated and fortified for good measure, the Tour Bonbec (right in the photo) has origins as old as the Palais de la Cité. It contained a "questioning chamber" where tongues were loosened, prisoners confessing even more quickly when aided by various forms of tortures.

The armory.

Pont Neuf and Place Dauphine

1st ARRONDISSEMENT

Square du Vert-Galant at the tip of the Île-de-la-Cité.

From the king, against the king

The statue of Henri IV on the Pont Neuf was knocked down during the Revolution, as were all representations of sovereigns. In 1818, a new equestrian statue—the one we see today—replaced that which disappeared. A recent restoration revealed that the work contains anti-royalist pamphlets, which a Bonapartist chiseler placed in the statue. He wanted to protest the fact the statue was created from bronze from melted statues of Napoleon.

The Pont Neuf, the "new bridge", was aptly named when it was completed in 1607; today it is the oldest bridge in Paris. When it was built, though, it was not only new, but also original—it was the first stone bridge in the city and the first to be built without houses on either side, as was the custom. The Parisians won a real balcony on the Seine and appreciated the perspective, to the point of making it the crossroads of city life. Wide, high sidewalks protected pedestrians from traffic hazards, allowing them to wander at their leisure. Always lively, hawkers' stalls proliferated on the bridge, which succeeded brick-and-mortar shops in the corbels, while hawkers, charlatans, animal tamers, jugglers and comedians on trestles competed for the attention of onlookers. These audiences were prime targets for thieves of all kinds, who were very active in the area.

While Henri IV had to content himself with inaugurating the Pont Neuf despite not being its originator, the creation of the Place Dauphine—in honor of the dauphin, the future Louis XIII, then aged six—was completely his decision. The king offered Parisians the new bridge and was already engaged in work on the Place Royale (later called Place des Vosges). The second royal square returned to the principle of uniformity, with thirty-two identical brick-and-stone houses covered with slate built on three sides. Today the original facades remain on only two pavilions overlooking the Pont Neuf; the other buildings have been demolished or heavily reworked. The row facing Rue de Harlay was razed in 1874 to reveal the Palais de Justice's new facade, which was at that time considered to be the main entrance.

Place Dauphine.

The piers of the Pont Neuf.

Île-Saint-Louis
4th ARRONDISSEMENT

Formed in the seventeenth century by the meeting of the Île Notre-Dame and the Île aux Vaches, ithe Île-Saint-Louis saw its urbanization entrusted, in 1614, to a trio of entrepreneurs: Christophe Marie and his associates, Lugles Poulletier and François Le Regrattier had to stabilize the land, develop the waterfront and link the new island with the two banks and its neighbor, the Île-de-la-Cité.
The work, however, dragged on, and the team was soon replaced by another, who enlisted the architectural services of the Le Vau brothers. The Rue Saint-Louis-en-l'Île was mapped as the development's backbone, onto which secondary arteries were grafted at right angles. After a few years, beautiful buildings and townhouses appeared. The new district did not downgrade the aristocratic Marais, but attracted parliamentarians and the nouveaux riches.
Louis Le Vau, future architect of Vaux-le-Vicomte, particularly distinguished himself with the remarkable Hôtel Lambert and the Hôtel Lauzun on the Quai d'Anjou. Painter Charles Le Brun, whose work could be found in royal residences, enhanced the Hôtel Lambert's gallery, while the Hôtel Lauzun has maintained its spectacular interiors dripping with gold. In the 1840s, the latter opened to tenants, among them Charles Baudelaire and Théophile Gautier. Both frequented the Club des Hashischins, established at the same address, enjoying this artificial paradise in the company of Eugène Delacroix, Gustave Flaubert, Gérard de Nerval, Alexandre Dumas, and many other bohemians from the artistic and literary worlds.

Quai d'Orléans

The Quays of the Seine

Long confined to the purely utilitarian role of a waterway or open sewer, in the early seventeenth century the Seine was discovered anew by Parisians as an ornamental pond. The city that had turned its back on the river turned once more to enjoy the scenery, the view over the river, and marked its banks with monuments and beautiful townhouses. The undertaking would continue over the centuries, with the Seine becoming the city's major architectural axis. The development of the quays regularized its course and facilitated access that the buildings constructed directly above the river's edge prohibited.

The Pont Neuf was the first bridge to not have houses, and new works followed suit. On the eve of the Revolution, the king ordered the destruction of the homes that were still on Paris's old bridges.

By the beginning of the Grand Siècle, as the reign of Louis XIV is known, the city had five bridges: by the end of the Ancien Régime that number had doubled, and in the nineteenth century twenty more were added. In 1891, the first green boxes of the *bouquqinistes*, the booksellers, appeared on the Quai Voltaire, increasingly populating the quays to such an extent they somehow became a symbol of them.

Today, thirty-four bridges and four footbridges cross the Seine in its Parisian course. Since 1991, a long area, running from the Pont de Sully to the Pont d'Iéna and the Pont de Bir-Hakeim on the Left Bank, including the Île-de-la-Cité and the Île-Saint-Louis, have been part of UNESCO's world heritage list. Recently, the Left Bank quays from the Musée d'Orsay to the Pont de l'Alma, have been for the exclusive use of pedestrians, offering more than two kilometers of tranquil wanderings beside the water, punctuated by fun activities, creative workshops and refreshments. The Right Bank has not been left out: each summer, near Hôtel de Ville, it hosts Paris Plages.

The Quay of the Balconies

That was how the Quai de Bethune was known before it adopted the name of one of Henri IV's ministers. Indeed Louis le Vau had recommended that all townhouses likely to enjoy a view of the Seine have a balcony. This recent invention first appeared in Paris around 1640, at the Place Royal (today the Place des Vosges) and the large mansions of the Île-Saint-Louis, Bretonvilliers (now gone except for its pavilion) and Lambert.

The Pont and Quai de la Tournelle.

The *bouquinistes*, Quai des Grands-Augustins.

The Pont Marie, in front of the Pont Louis-Philippe.

Place des Vosges

3rd AND 4th ARRONDISSEMENTS

This was the site of the royal residence, the Palais des Tournelles: in July 1559 Henri II died here, from injuries received during a tournament. His widow, Catherine de Médicis, abandoned the palace and eventually had it destroyed. Later, in order to boost the Parisian economy, Henri IV established a silk factory on the site. In 1605, he wanted to give the silk trade more majesty and so he had the square lined with identical brick-and-stone houses. Place Royale was born, with a promising future, but the silk trade declined rapidly and the factory was destroyed.

Within a few years, the north bank was subdivided into nine pavilions, similar to those of the other three sides with the exception of the queen's pavilion, which was higher than its neighbors, replicating the king's pavilion it faced. Inaugurated in 1612, the square hosted the theater festival celebrating the betrothal of Louis XIII to Anne of Austria. The nobles attending these festivities helped promote  the square and it was soon occupied by aristocrats. The site retained its prestige, despite the changing fashions in real estate.

The Revolution scattered the noble families and seized many properties. Thus from 1800, a more middle-class population could be seen under the arcades, while the square became "des Vosges" to signal the civic virtue of the first department to pay its taxes.

Of the many Parisians who chose to live at the square, the most illustrious was Victor Hugo, who lived there from 1832–48, at number 6. Today it is home to the museum dedicated to this great man.

The orderly architecture of the Place des Vosges from the central square.

The equestrian statue of Louis XIII.

Hôtel de Sully

48 RUE SAINT-ANTOINE (4th)

This townhouse, reached via its garden from the Place des Vosges, carries the name of Henri IV's great minister who became its owner in 1634, when he was already an elderly man. Nevertheless, he was committed to improving the decor of his new home, which remained in the Sully family until the mid-eighteenth century. In the nineteenth century, the residence, like many in the Marais, was transformed into an investment property and housed craftsmen's workshops and shops, adulterating the site. It was bought by the state in 1944, and after a long period of restoration, regained its splendor.

The Hôtel de Sully's main courtyard.

In the main courtyard, the statue of Louis XIV by Antoine Coysevox.

Musée Carnavalet

16 RUE DES FRANCS-BOURGEOIS (3ᵗʰ)

Built in the mid-sixteenth century, this townhouse was among the first in the Marais. It remains one of the rare Parisian vestiges of Renaissance secular architecture. We can particularly admire its main facade, with its bas reliefs of the Four Seasons, created by the sculptor Jean Goujon, who was also responsible for the works in the Carrée du Louvre's courtyard and the Fountain of the Innocents. Twenty years after its construction, the house was bought by the widow of a Breton gentleman, Françoise Kernevenoy. Parisians altered his unpronounceable surname to "Carnavalet," and the name remained even when it was home to the more illustrious Madame de Sévigné between 1677 and 1694. In her "Carnavalette," the letter writer held her salon and, above all, wrote, including to her daughter, with whom she exchanged more than a thousand letters. Reflecting an era and a society, this correspondence not only provides a chronicle but gives a picture of the spirit and the mood. The marquise was living in a very different home from the original version, since in the mid-seventeenth century François Mansart had been instructed to enlarge the space and update the decor. The great architect replaced the broken roof, changed the left wing and the entrance porch, and added a wing to the right of the main section.

The city of Paris acquired the building in 1866, to transform it into a museum of the city, housing its historical collections. For the occasion, the main courtyard welcomed the beautiful statue of Louis XIV from the Hôtel de Ville.

Marie de Rabutin-Chantal, Marquise de Sévigné, by Claude Lefèbvre, c. 1665.

The staircase from the old Hôtel de Luynes.

The Cour de la Victoire is home to the Winged Victory that came from the Fontaine du Châtelet.

Paradoxically, at a time when the Second Empire and the prefect Haussmann began to tear down large parts of Old Paris, the city acquired the Hôtel Carnavalet to house a museum dedicated to the capital's history. The institution opened in 1880, expanded in 1900 and again in 1989, by annexing the neighboring Hôtel Le Peletier de Saint-Fargeau. It is in the latter's former orangery that the famous canoes, over six thousand years old, found at Bercy, are displayed.

The collections shown at the Carnavalet cover a wide period of time, from Neolithic to the twentieth century. Paintings, models, everyday and ceremonial objects, furniture, signs, and more lead visitors through the centuries.

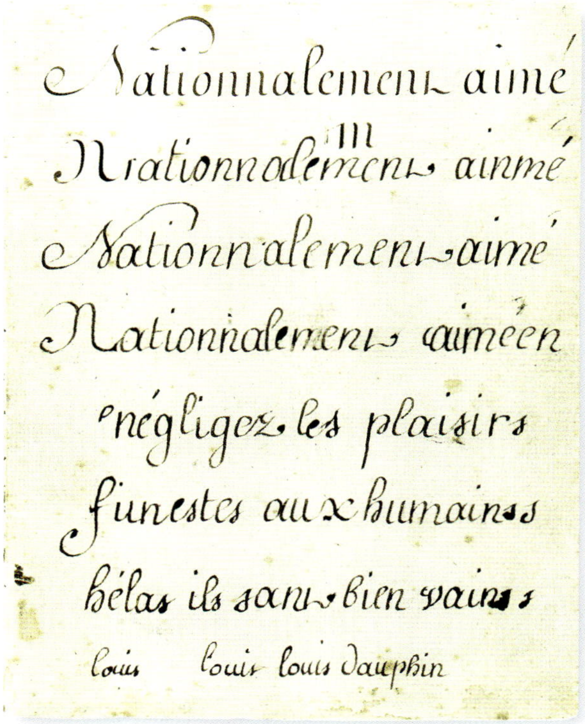

Gallic money: Parisii Stater.

A page written by the dauphin during his incarceration in the dungeon of the Temple in 1793. Lovers of old things are completely immersed in history, discovering a stunning seventeenth-century living room and a mansion's sumptuous Art Deco ballroom. Other pieces offer the chance to enter into the intimate world of a writer's room: here we have Marcel Proust, Paul Léautaud and Anna de Noailles, whose furniture has been carefully placed in reproductions of their original decors. Further along, we contemplate a completely different interior, stopping in front of the reconstitution of the royal family's cell at the Temple prison during the Revolution. Louis XVI was held there until ascending to the guillotine in September 1792, and Marie Antoinette until her turn in October. The dauphin, who became Louis XVII after his father's execution, did not meet the same fate, and died in the Temple in June 1795. At the beginning of his imprisonment, the seven-year old conscientiously completed pages of writing under the watch of his parents; we see a poignant example on the wall.

Sign from the cabaret, Le Chat Noir.

Page written by the dauphin during his stay at the Temple prison.

Neolithic canoe, found in pieces in the east of Paris.

Louis XV's Blue Salon: paneling from the Hôtel Brulart de Genlis (c. 1780).

Cradle of the crown prince, Louis-Napoléon.

Old apothecary window.

A scale model of the Bastille cut from one of the prison's stones.

Musée National Picasso-Paris

5 RUE DE THORIGNY (3rd)

One of the sphinxes standing guard outside the entrance.

The museum occupies the Hôtel Aubert de Fontenay, built in 1659, best known as the Hôtel Salé ("Salty"). That is how the Parisians called it, alluding to the fortune of its owner, a *gabelle* collecter, the tax on salt under the Ancien Régime. After various lives, the building was converted to house the Musée Picasso, which opened its doors in 1985. Its holdings are made up of Picasso's personal collection, rich in canvases by Matisse, Braque, Miró, Chardin, Cézanne, among others, gifts from the master's inheritors and the legacy of Jacqueline Roque, his last wife. In total, the museum houses three hundred paintings, more than two hundred sculptures, around a hundred ceramics, thousands of drawings and tens of thousands various documents. An exceptional synthesis of the work of this genius of painting, the museum allows contemplation of major paintings, including *La Celestine*, *Portrait of Dora Maar*, the *Pipes of Pan* and *Man with Guitar*. The sculptures exhibited include *Woman in the Garden*, *She-Goat*, the *Bull's Head* and the *Monkey and Her Baby*. Through casts, bronzes and photographs by Brassaï, the basement evokes the various workshops where Picasso worked.

The facade on the Hôtel Salé's courtyard.

The room dedicated to Cézanne was formerly an attic.

Two sculptures by Picasso, with the *She-Goat* (1950) in the foreground.

Centre Pompidou
PLACE GEORGES-POMPIDOU (4th)

When it opened its doors in 1977, in the heart of Old Paris, this still-hard-to-identify architectural object was described as a "refinery" or a "gas factory" by some critics. Since then the institution generally referred to as "Beaubourg," in reference to its neighborhood, has blended into the landscape and, above all, into traditions, each year attracting more than five million visitors to the public library and the national modern art museum it houses. The collections of the latter represent all of the art movements of the twentieth and twenty-first centuries: more than a hundred thousand works of which some two thousand from around seven hundred artists are displayed in rotation. Generally chronological, the visit begins with representatives of Fauvism, including Matisse, Vlaminck and Derain, the Cubism of Picasso and Braque, the Futurists, the Surrealists, and the School of Paris illustrated by Chagall, Modigliani and Soutine. The proponents of Abstract Expressionism follow, Pollock and Rothko, the lyrical Staël and Soulanges, the painters of the Cobra movement, Pop Art, Minimalism and the disciples of Arte Povera. Alongside its permanent collection, the Centre Pompidou offers temporary exhibitions, which in recent years have included retrospectives of Jeff Koons and Salvador Dali that broke all attendance records: 800,000 people rushed through the tubing of the temple to modern and contemporary art.

Nothing to hide
The center's architects, Renzo Piano and Richard Rogers, took the daring step of showing what architecture usually hides. Thus the supporting structure and the pipes are outside, highlighted by vibrant colors: blue corresponds to air supply, yellow to electrical devices and red to the elevators and their machinery.

Stravinsky Fountain

Artist Niki de Saint Phalle and sculptor Jean Tinguely created the population of this almost six-hundred-square-meter fountain built in 1983. Sixteen of their works, in black metal or colored resin, inhabit the pond bordering the northern section of the Church of Saint-Merri. Through jets of water, these machines perform a fascinating ballet. All refer to the work of Russian composer Igor Stravinsky, beginning with the *Firebird*, which dominates the fountain.

Hôtel de Soubise

60 RUE DES FRANCS-BOURGEOIS (3rd)

Open onto Rue des Francs-Bourgeois, a huge colonnaded courtyard underlines the majesty of this building and the status of its owner: at the beginning of the eighteenth century, this was François de Rohan, Prince de Soubise. For over two centuries the hotel housed the national archives, and today it is home to its museum.

Hôtel de Sens

1 RUE DU FIGUIER (4ᵗʰ)

Tristan de Salazar, Archbishop of Sens, built the townhouse between the late fifteenth century and the early sixteenth century. Along with the Hôtel de Cluny, it is one of the oldest *hôtels particuliers*, or townhouses, in Paris. It is perhaps best known for its famous resident, the turbulent Queen Margot, who lived there after the annulment of her marriage to Henri IV. Today it is home to the Bibliothèque Forney.

Saint-Paul-Saint-Louis church

99 RUE SAINT-ANTOINE (4th)

Situated in the heart of the great aristocratic quarter of the seventeenth century, the Saint-Paul-Saint-Louis church opened its doors in 1641 to an assembly of handpicked parishioners. Cardinal Richelieu celebrated the first Mass on May 9 of that year. Here, throughout the Grand Siècle, religious service reached a summit, with its organs under the direction of music master Marc-Antoine Charpentier and confessions heard by the Jesuits, who were the spiritual directors of the kings.

The sermons of Louis Bourdaloue and of Jacques-Bénigne Bossuet attracted considerable crowds: for those of Bourdaloue it was prudent to send your valet at 3 pm to hold your place for five hours! Madame de Sévigné confided that she was "transported" by his funeral oration for Louis de Bourbon, Prince of Condé, of whom he said: "He surpassed himself, and that is saying a lot." After the Revolution, during which five priests were killed in the church, the building returned to being a house of worship and rediscovered its high-society congregation. Victor Hugo's daughter Léopoldine was married there in 1843. His sons had also been baptized there, and the writer was the one who gave the church the huge shells that still serve as the fonts at the entrance.

Wall of Philippe Augustus

Behind Saint-Paul-Saint-Louis and along the Rue des Jardins-Saint-Paul is the most important trace of the wall called Philippe Augustus. Before leaving on the Third Crusade in the early twelfth century, the sovereign wished to protect Paris behind ramparts. In this 120-meter section, a few pieces remain, miraculously preserved by finding themselves integrated into ordinary housing: when the buildings along Rue des Jardins-Saint-Paul were destroyed in 1946, they were revealed, intact!

Hôtel de Ville

PLACE DE L'HÔTEL-DE-VILLE (4th)

Coat of arms of the city of Paris.

At the height of the Middle Ages, this was a port, its gently sloping shoreline dubbed Port de Grève (Beach Port). By extension, the square prolonging it inherited the name. And it was on the Place de Grève in 1357, that Étienne Marcel, the merchants' provost established the first municipal government in one of the buildings bordering the square, the Maison aux Piliers, so named because of its pillared arcades on the ground floor. This first Hôtel de Ville (city hall) was succeeded by another, in the mid-sixteenth century, designed by the great Italian architect Boccador in the style of the Renaissance. Finished at the beginning of the Grand Siècle, the Hôtel de Ville burned in the fires of the Semaine Sanglante (the Bloody Week), the final espisode of the Paris Commune, in May 1871. A resolution to remake the building from its ruins was taken, expanding and upgrading it to better meet the needs of the time, while drawing heavily from—to the point of copying—the original facade. A hundred statues depict famous men, all born in Paris, with the notable exception of Boccador. As he had to give a face to someone whose visage was unknown to him, the sculptor chose to offer him the traits of Théodore Ballu, architect of the reconstructed building! Inside, a large ballroom stretching over fifty meters is reminiscent of the Hall of Mirrors at the Château de Versailles.

On strike

To be *en grève* in French is to be "on strike," a right workers passionately believe in. The Place de Grève hosted large city festivals, but also public executions ... which sometimes amounted to the same thing! It was also on this square that workers eager to be hired would gather; occasionally, they would go *en grève* to bring their grievances to the attention of the city fathers. Thus the expression *être en grève* referred to the situation of a worker without work before taking on the sense that we now know.

Ceiling of the Salon des Arts.

Place du Châtelet

1ST AND 4TH ARRONDISSEMENTS

One of the Fontaine du Palmier's four sphinxes, sculpted by Henri-Alfred Jacquemart.

Tour Saint-Jacques
39 RUE DE RIVOLI (4th)

The tower is the sole trace of the Saint-Jacques-de-la-Boucherie church, destroyed in 1797. It was the church's bell tower and among its various functions, it was host to Blaise Pascal's physics experiments and provided a landmark for pilgrims of the Camino de Santiago. Haussman assigned to it the privilege of being the first Parisian square's picturesque ornament, as well as being the symbol of the *grande croisée*, the great crossing of modern Paris, which he created with the Boulevard de Sébastopol and Rue de Rivoli based on the Roman model of a *cardo* (north-south) and a *decumanus* (east-west) axes.

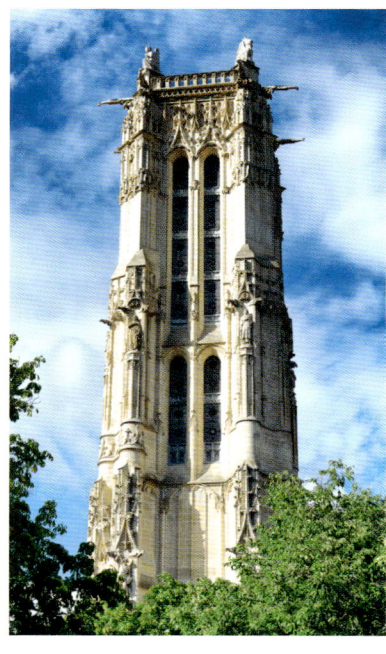

Nothing remains of the Grand Châtelet, built in the High Middle Ages to protect the Grand Pont and the Île-de-la-Cité, home to the heart of Paris and the Palais-Royal. When the Châtelet lost its defensive interest, it became a prison, which was razed in the early nineteenth century to develop the current square. This is decorated with the Egyptian-influenced Fontaine du Palmier, installed in 1806, which has the particularity of having been moved several meters in 1856; the placement of Boulevard de Sébastopol and the remodeling of the square at the time of the Hausmanization led to the move 12 meters so that the fountain could remain at the square's center. The operation, which consisted of gliding the monument as a unit, on rails, took ten minutes before an amazed crowd.

On either side of the square, the Théâtre du Châtelet and the Théâtre de la Ville were built, both in 1862 by the architect Gabriel Davioud.

Place des Victoires

1st AND 2nd ARRONDISSEMENTS

The Place des Victoires is, or rather was, the epitome of a royal square, as were the Vosges and Dauphine squares before it. Closed in on themselves, they are not intended to open onto a monumental perspective, but provide a setting for the statue of the monarch: here, Louis XIV. The project was initially financed by François de la Feuillade, a marshal of France and vicomte d'Aubusson, but was taken over by the Bâtiments de Roi and entrusted to the royal architect, Jules Hardouin-Mansart. The architect took care to calculate the radius of the place accorded to the sculpted work to ensure that no street is facing another.
Thus royal effigies would be detached from their backgrounds, not part of the landscape. However, in 1883, the reconstruction of most of the buildings surrounding the square altered the original regularity and cut the Rue Étienne-Marcel, damaging Hardouin-Mansart's creation. The square has long lost its statue and its status. Indeed in 1792, the Revolution melted the king's bronze. He was later replaced by a Roman-style nude of General Desaix, hero of the Battle of Marengo, who died for the homeland at the age of thirty-one. Under the Restoration, this symbol had its turn in the foundry to be turned into the statue of Henri IV on the Pont Neuf, while Louis XIV on horseback conquered the center of the Place des Victoires.

Saint-Germain-l'Auxerrois
2 PLACE DU LOUVRE (1st)
This was once the parish of the kings of France, the church of the Louvre. We also know that it was the bells of Saint-Germain that on August 24, 1572 sounded the signal for the Saint Bartholomew's Day massacre. Deconsecrated and sacked under the Revolution, the church was restored in the mid-nineteenth century. Haussmann chose to mirror the church's facade in the neighboring town hall of the 1st arrondissement.

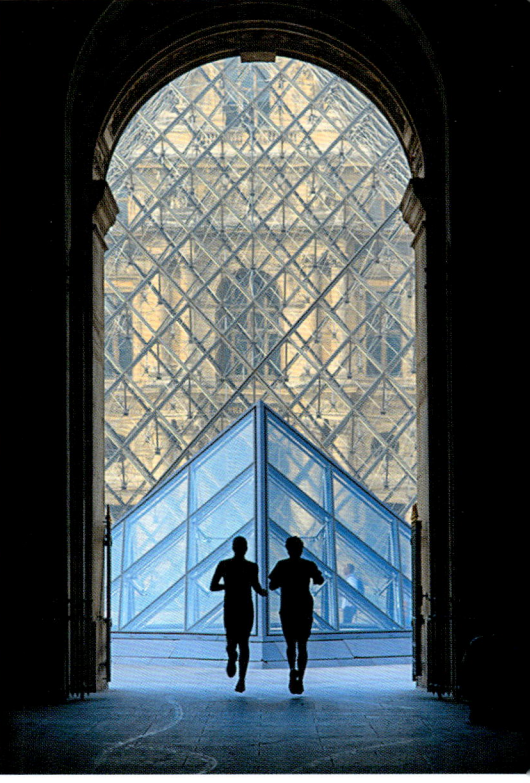

Palais du Louvre

1st ARRONDISSEMENT

The foundations of the medieval Louvre.

The statue of Rabelais, by Elias Robert, between the Cour Napoléon and Rue de Rivoli.

Before becoming a museum or even a palace, the Louvre was a fortress, constructed at the end of the twelfth century by Philippe Augustus, with the intention that the enclosure would protect Paris. The building was presented as a massive keep protected by curtain walls flanked by towers and a moat.

The keep housed the royal treasury, and was, on occasion, used as a prison. It was another monarch, Charles V, who made the Louvre more pleasant and more comfortable. Creating windows, laying out the garden and installing a library, the king transformed a military construction into an agreeable residence.

But it was François I who made the most radical transformation, razing the old keep to build a new, Renaissance-style castle. His successors continued along the same lines, giving the palace the same dimensions as the Cour Carrée, four times larger than the medieval Louvre. At the very beginning of the seventeenth century, Henri IV built the Galerie du Bord-de-l'Eau to connect the Louvre with the Palais des Tuileries. Louis XIV finished the work on the Cour Carrée and endowed the "facade facing the city with a colonnade, before deciding to move to Versailles. Finally it was Napoleon III who finalized the "grand design," connecting the Louvre and the Tuileries. This was effected by the installation of Elias Robert's statue of Rabelais between the Cour Napoléon and Rue de Rivoli. This figure, though, only remained for a short time, lost in the fires of the Commune, which destroyed the Palais des Tuileries in June 1871. We can read the Louvre like a history book: the foundations of the medieval fortress are visible in the basement; the Cour Carrée is the result of the work between the reigns of François I and Louis XIV; the wings of the Cour Napoléon were opened during the Second Empire, and frame I.M. Pei's famous pyramid, symbol of the Grand Louvre, refurbished in the twentieth century.

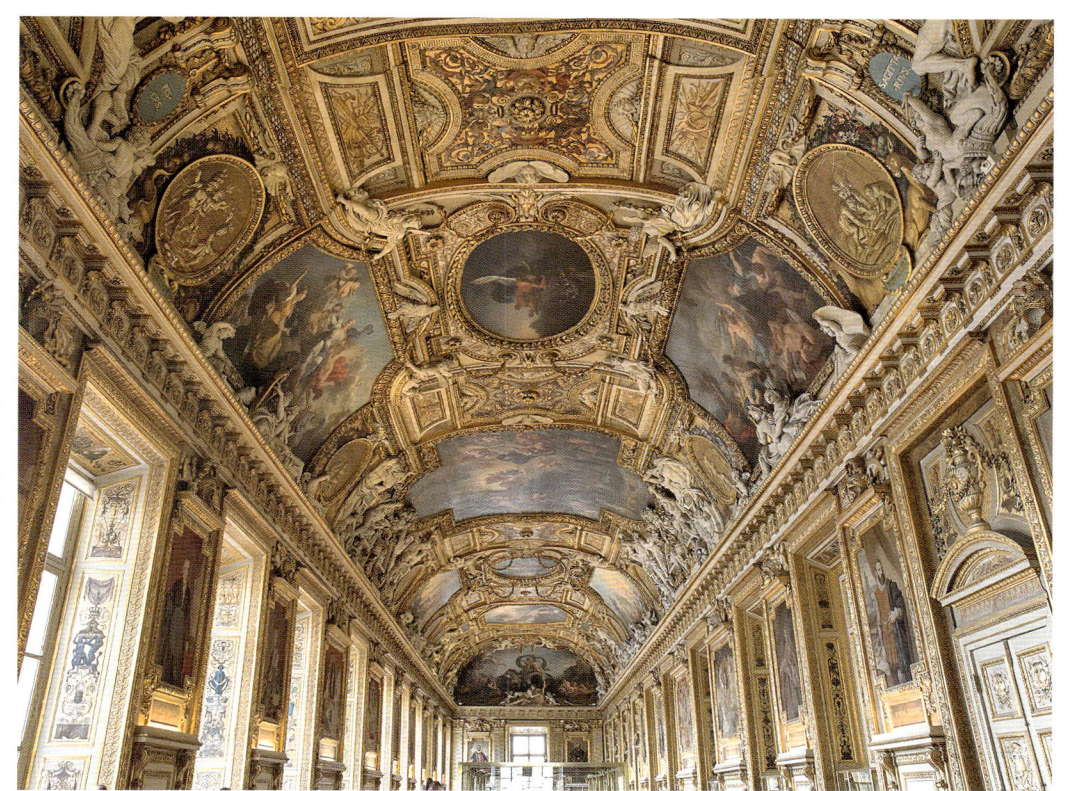

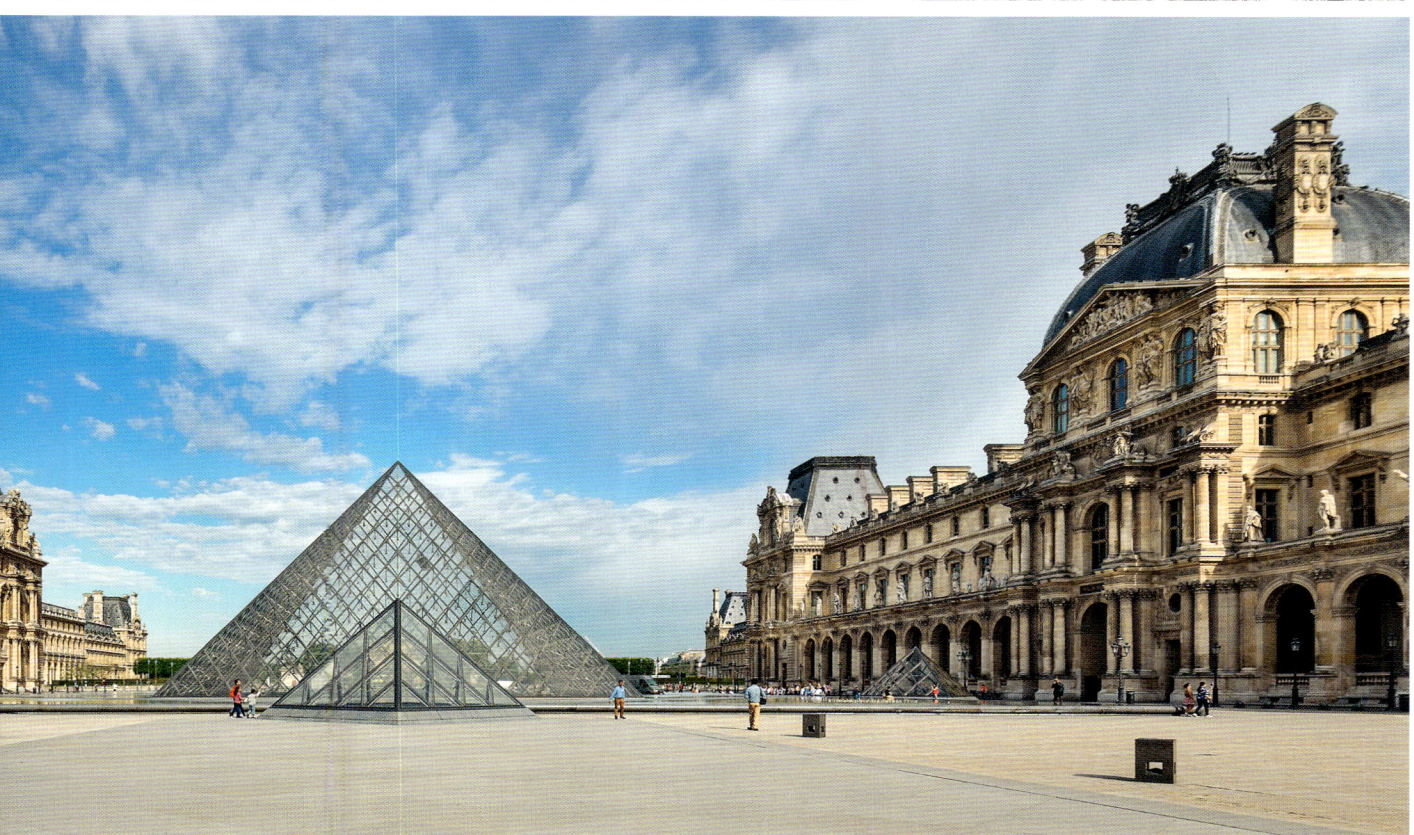

The Cour Napoléon.

Colonnade giving onto the Rue de l'Amiral-de-Coligny.

Musée du Louvre

1st ARRONDISSEMENT

Sitting Scribe.

An honorary member of the exclusive club of the world's greatest museums, the Louvre is the busiest, the bar set at ten million visitors a year, and that's not counting the numbers that visit the antenna museum in Lens, in northern France. Plans to open the remarkable royal collections to the public took shape under the Ancien Régime, though it was not until the Revolution that the plan was fulfilled. On November 8, 1793, the Muséum Central des Arts de la République welcomed its first visitors to the Grande Galerie du Louvre. The paintings came from the king's collections or from religious institutions that had been declared national property and aristocrats' residences that had been requisitioned. Soon added to these were works of art pillaged in Belgium and Italy by the Republique's victorious army. The young General Bonaparte organized the large shipments. He was First Consul when the museum was renamed the Musée Napoléon. Emptied of the artists and other tenants that lived in its salons and corridors, it was redeveloped to accommodate the booty of military campaigns.

At the fall of the Empire, the Louvre returned the seized works. Collections were now made up of only acquisitions and donations. This was the case for the *Venus de Milo*, offered by the Marquis de Rivière to Louis XVIII in 1821. In the mid-nineteenth century, the *Seated Scribe*, found by the Egyptologist Auguste Mariette eclipsed the previously uncontested star, the *Mona Lisa*, which came from the collections of François I, and traveled from Fontainebleau to Versailles and the Tuileries, at the mercy of the changing residences of successive sovereigns. It as not until the early

Human-headed winged bull from Mesopotamia.

The Cour Puget.

Winged Victory of Samothrace.

nineteenth century that the world's most famous portrait found its way to the walls of the Louvre. From the beginning, the *Mona Lisa* has fascinated poets, writers, artists and fanatics of all sorts ... including Vincenzo Peruggia, who successfully stole the painting in August 1911 and hid it for more than two years, triggering a case that saw Guillaume Apollinaire and Pablo Picasso arrested for the crime (and subsequently released), and which made the space vacated by the painting more visited than the grand lady herself previously had been, making the painting the most famous the world has ever known.

Venus de Milo.

Joan of Arc, by François Rude, 1852.

Mona Lisa – Portrait of Lisa Gherardini, Wife of Francesco del Giocondo, by Leonardo da Vinci, c. 1503–06.

The Raft of the Medusa, by Théodore Géricault, 1819.

Portrait of the Artist Holding a Thistle, by Albrecht Dürer, 1493.

The Cheat with the Ace of Diamonds, by Georges de La Tour, 1635.

The Lacemaker, by Johannes Vermeer, 1669–70.

Palais-Royal

8 RUE DE MONTPENSIER (1st)

Built and occupied by the Duc de Richelieu, the palace was first called "Cardinal," but became the Palais-Royal when passed to the crown. Anne of Austria lived there with her young son, the future Louis XIV, before the Fronde—the civil wars between the king and, at various times between 1648 and 1653, the princes, nobles and the parliaments—incited the young king to flee in 1649, and then after his return, to have rioters invade his room in 1651. On succeeding to the throne, Louis was not interested in the residence, and turned it over to his brother and his descendants.

The site then enjoyed a glittering period, during which an enlightened aristocratic society—as interested in the arts as in games and other pleasures—held "Palais-Royal suppers." Destroyed by a fire in 1763, the Palais-Royal was mostly rebuilt. The last owner/occupier before the Revolution, Louis-Philippe d'Orléans subdivided shops and homes around the edge of the garden to ensure a regular income, in the hope of covering the considerable debts he had accumulated. The Théâtre du Palais-Royal was rebuilt at the same time as work on the Théâtre-Français and the Cirque du Palais-Royal, in the middle of the garden. The site then became the center for Parisian entertainment, drawing huge crowds in search of elegance, entertainment and pleasure. The ban on police, by princely privilege, allowed the flourishing of much trade, starting with gaming and prostitution.

Ideas also circulated freely; it was here that the scene signaling the start of the Revolution unfolded. On July 12, 1789, Camille Desmoulins jumped on a table and called for an insurrection. The Ancien Régime fell, and the Palais Royal became the Palais-Égalité, but remained the crossroads of Parisian pleasures. It was only in the 1830s that the gambling houses closed and the prostitutes left. Today the Palais Royal is much calmer. It houses the Council of State, and on the Rue de Valois, the Ministry of Culture.

Daniel Buren's columns in the main courtyard.

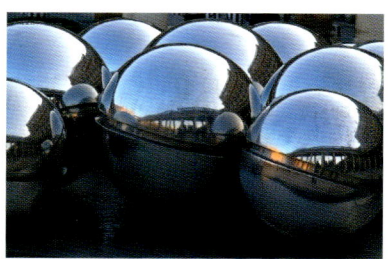

Fountain by Pol Bury.

In the gardens, the *Snake Charmer*, by Adolphe Thabard, 1875.

The Jardin des Tuileries
113 RUE DE RIVOLI (1st)

The Octagonal Fountain.

Cain after Killing his Brother, by Henri Vidal, 1896.

The Jardin des Tuileries carries a shadow of what has disappeared; it bears the name of the palace that Catherine de Médicis built in 1564, which she had embellished with compartmentalized garden beds in the Italian fashion. A century later, Louis XIV entrusted the garden to André Le Nôtre, and his design gave the garden the configuration we know today, with the large central pathway, punctuated by two fountains, and the Des Feuillants and Bord-de l'Eau terraces, and the ramps on the side of the main entrance, Place de la Concorde. The other side of the garden, its western extremity, is home to two museums, L'Orangerie and the Jeu de Paume. The first was built in 1853, ensuring its name was known before being designated as the best setting for Claude Monet's *Water Lilies*, his gift to France. Beyond this iconic work, the museum now offers a wider panorama of Impressionist and Post-Impressionist painting. The second building, housing the Jeu de Paume, is a counterpoint to the first. During the Occupation, it was used as storage for works stolen by the Nazis before being shipped to Germany. After the Liberation, the museum renewed its vocation, and since 2004, it has hosted exhibitions of video and photographic work. To the east of the Jardin des Tuileries, on the other side of Avenue du Général-Lemonnier, lie the Jardins du Carrousel where around twenty generously curved Aristide Maillol statues emerge from the hedges. Further toward the Louvre is the Arc de Triomphe du Carrousel, built in 1809 by Napoleon, in honor of the Grande Armée after the victory at Austerlitz. It was constructed as the gateway to the Palais des Tuileries, which was destroyed during the fires of the Commune in 1871, leaving the arch standing.

A sculpture by Aristide Maillol.

The large pond.

The Arc de Triomphe du Carrousel.

Musée du Jeu de Paume.

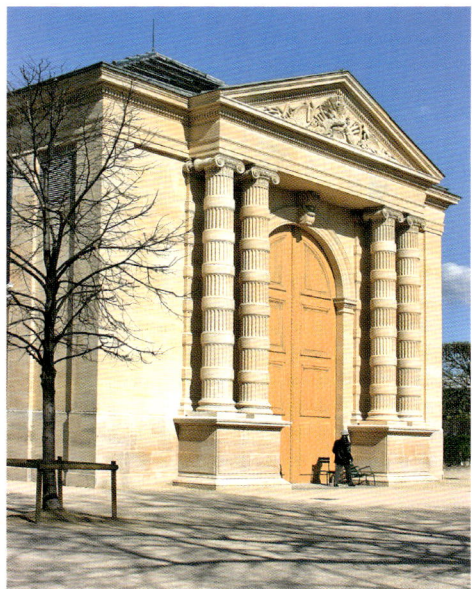

Musée de l'Orangerie.

The Roue de Paris.

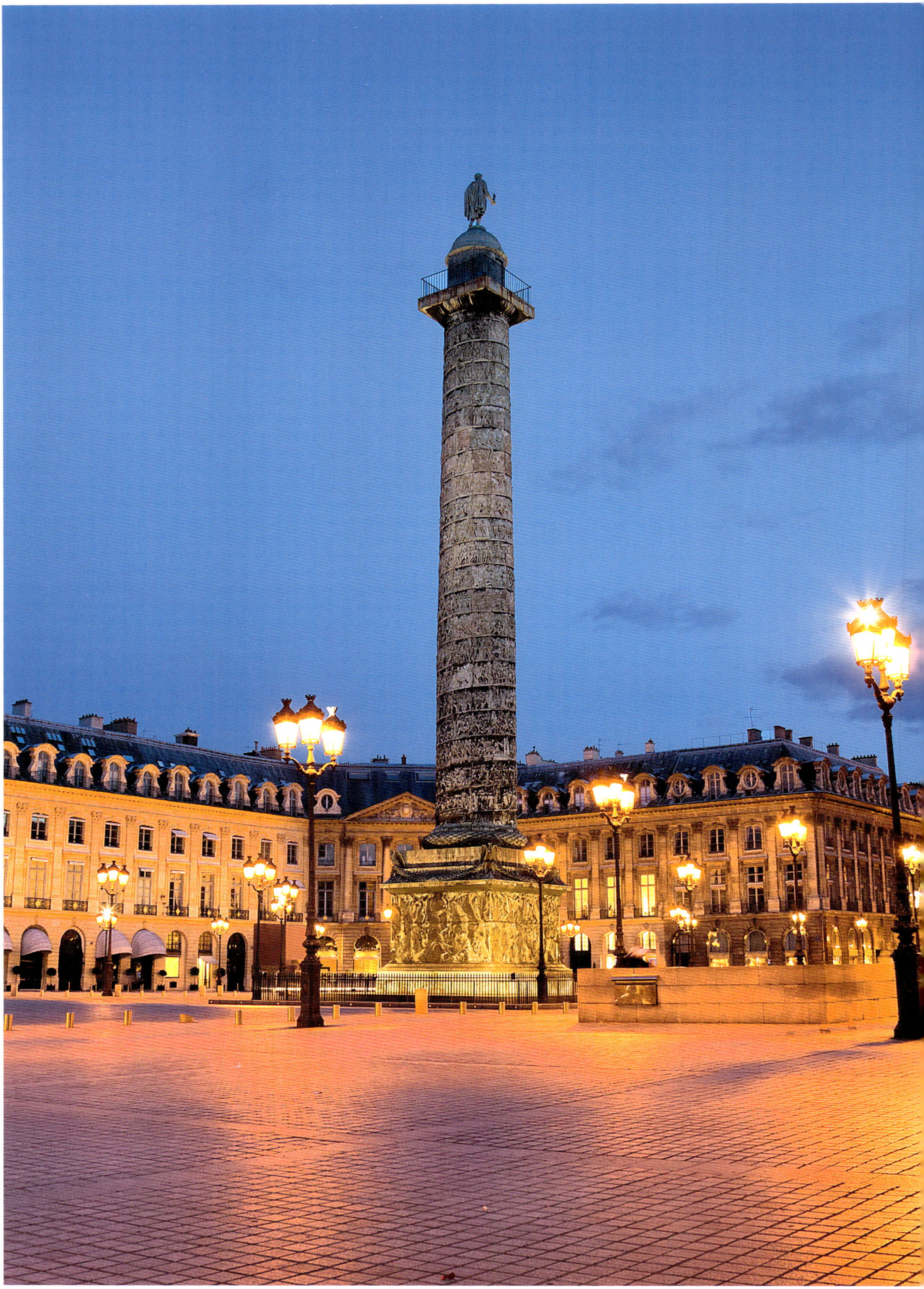

Place Vendôme

1st ARRONDISSEMENT

Place Louis-le-Grand was first conceived as a majestic quadrangle, lined with public buildings, to host the equestrian statue of Louis XIV. In 1699, for the square and the statue's inauguration, only the facades were built, the buildings themselves being put on hold. That same year, the king decided to sell the subdivision to a private initiative rather than use royal funds for the construction.

The facades were destroyed and architect Jules Hardouin-Mansart designed a new project: a canted square lined with townhouses, with identical facades, which would attract the Regency's financial elite and the aristocracy. The royal statue was destroyed during the Revolution, and in 1810 was replaced by the Vendôme column, which was cast in bronze from more than a thousand canons taken from the enemy. This replica of Trojan's column in Rome was topped by a representation of Napoleon as Caesar. With the fall of the Empire, however, the statue was taken down from its pedestal. It was not until 1833 and the July Monarchy that Napoleon returned to the top of the column, this time in military garb. Under the Second Empire, Napoleon III would provide his uncle with a Roman toga... but the Commune felled the column in 1871. The column and statue were raised once more, enjoying a peaceful life dominating the most elegant square in Paris. It was first a Mecca for fashion, before becoming more specialized in jewelry and luxury watches. Between Boucheron, Cartier, Chaumet, Van Cleef & Arpels, Piaget, Rolex, and more, there is hardly a number that isn't occupied by a renowned international name. Equally legendary of course is the Hôtel Ritz at number 15.

Napoleon as a Roman emperor.

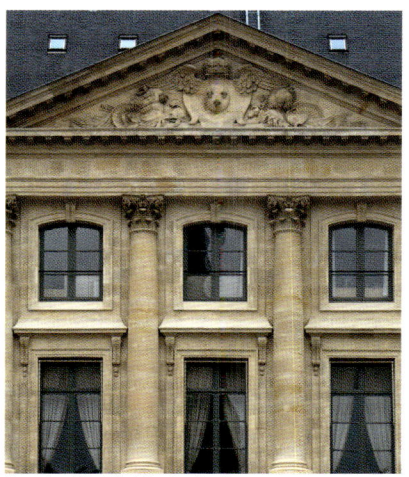

Facade of the Ministry for Justice.

The column is decorated in the antique manner, with bas-reliefs depicting battle scenes.

Palais-Bourbon, home to the National Assembly.

Place de la Concorde
8th ARRONDISSEMENT

An illustration of the idea that the biggest is the most beautiful! To spare public finances, Louis XV chose to develop the square on a site then outside the city. As opposed to the other royal Parisian squares, usually designed as settings around a statue of the monarch, Ange-Jacques Gabriel designed a mostly open space, bounded only on the north by two colonnaded palaces, which housed the Crown's furniture repository.

In the center was a statue of Louis XV, which was destroyed during the Revolution, while the guillotine was taking heads. Its scaffold was erected in the square, then called Révolution, and thousands mounted its platform there, including Louis XVI, then Marie Antoinette and later, Robespierre. To put the terrible memories behind, the square was renamed Place de la Concorde. It was redeveloped under the July Monarchy, carefully decorated in the most neutral way. In 1836, architect Jacques-Ignace Hittorff had the obelisk of the Temple of Luxor, a gift from the Viceroy of Egypt to France, erected

A detail on the obelisk.

in the center. Two large fountains were installed on either side, inspired by those in Saint Peter's Square in Rome. Statues of France's great cities surmounted the sentry boxes built by Gabriel. Finally, the interplay of the columns of the Palais-Bourbon on the Left Bank and those of the Madeleine church at the end of Rue Royale offer a perspective to the south and the north.

A detail from the square's fountains.

La Madeleine church on the Rue Royale.

The Grand and the Petit Palais

AVENUE WINSTON-CHURCHILL (8th)

The two palaces were designed together, as part of the 1900 World's Fair, with the intention of extending the perspective of the Invalides on the Right Bank. The Grand Palais took the place of the Palais de l'Industrie, which had been made for the 1855 Fair. More than two hundred meters long, the boldness of its huge glass roof and its metallic structure is striking, contrasting with the building's calm, academic countenance, a style of architecture typical of the Belle Époque. Since 1900, it has housed many artistic events, but also, since the early 1960s, exhibitions such as the Salon de l'Automibile and the book fair, the Salon du Livre. As well, the Grand Palais hosts temporary exhibitions, such as *Monumenta* and others that have attracted a particularly large audience: the record is held by the Monet exhibition, which attracted more than nine hundred thousand visitors during the winter of 2010.

Behind the exuberant ornamentation of its facade, the Petit Palais is home to the city of Paris's art and archaeological collections, which date from Antiquity to the late nineteenth century. It permanent collection as well as temporary exhibition attract a wide audience, but the long-standing record is for that of *Tutankhamun and His Time* in 1967, which attracted 1.2 million people!

The Pont Alexandre III cannot be dissociated from the Petit and the Grand Palais; it is contemporary with them, and is designed to give order to the perspective between the Champs-Élysées and Invalides. The bridge honors the friendship between Russia and France, and demonstrates the taste of 1900, as well as a technical feat, in crossing the Seine on a single arch.

The entrance to the Petit Palais, Musée des Beaux-Arts de la Ville de P

The Grand Palais from the Left Bank.

The statue of General de Gaulle, by Jean Cardot.

The Pont Alexandre III.

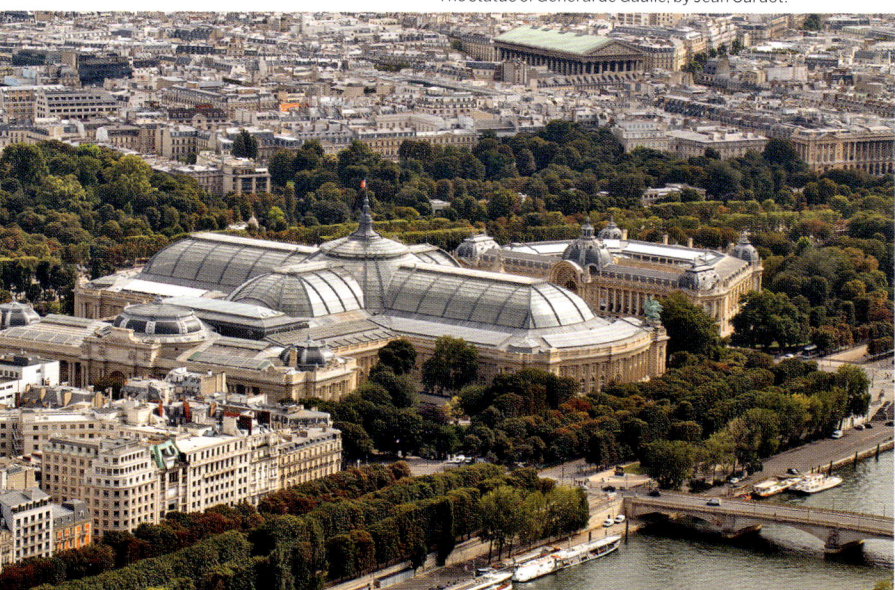

Aerial view of the Grand and Petit Palais.

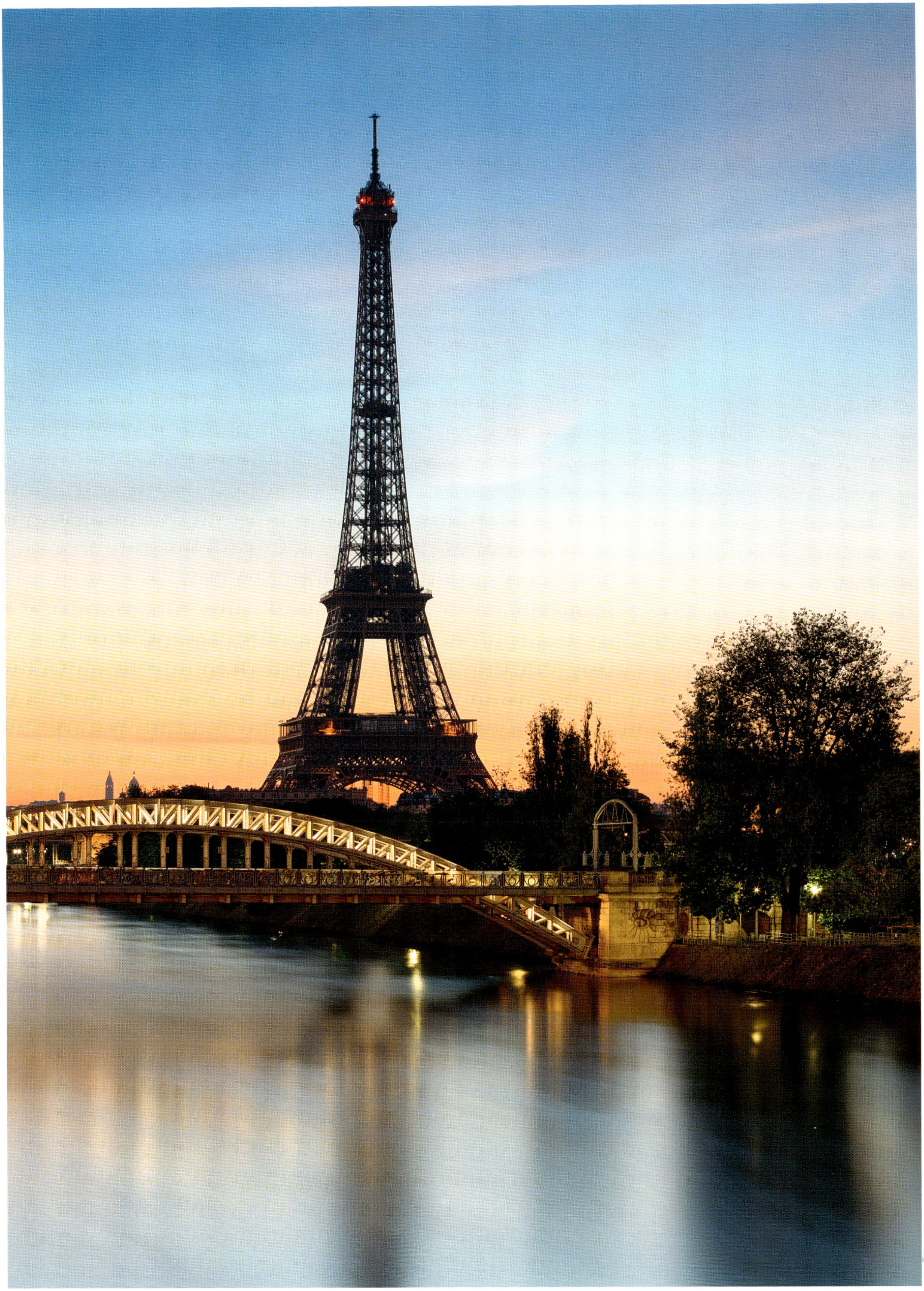

Eiffel Tower

5 AVENUE ANATOLE-FRANCE (7th)

Is there a more powerful symbol of Paris? The "300 meter tower," as it was first called, was erected in just over two years, to be the main attraction at the 1889 World's Fair. It held the record as the highest structure until 1930, when it was dethroned by New York's Chrysler Building. We know it was not Gustave Eiffel himself who designed the tower, but two of its engineers, but it was indeed Eiffel who focused on the project from start to finish, which enabled its completion, and its survival.

After the fair and the first wave of curiosity, the tower struggled to find its destiny; the possibility of its dismantling was considered. Gustave Eiffel tried to imagine a new function for the tower, and so financed wireless tests. The First World War made the importance of altitude for transmission clear. Thus its military use saved the tower, and its use extended in the 1920s with the broadcast of civilian radio programs and the first television trials. It was for television broadcasting that a new antenna was placed at the top in 1959, pushing the height to 321 meters. The development of tourism after the Second World War earned renewed attendance: with seven million ascendants annually, it is Paris's second-most visited site for paying visitors behind the Louvre.

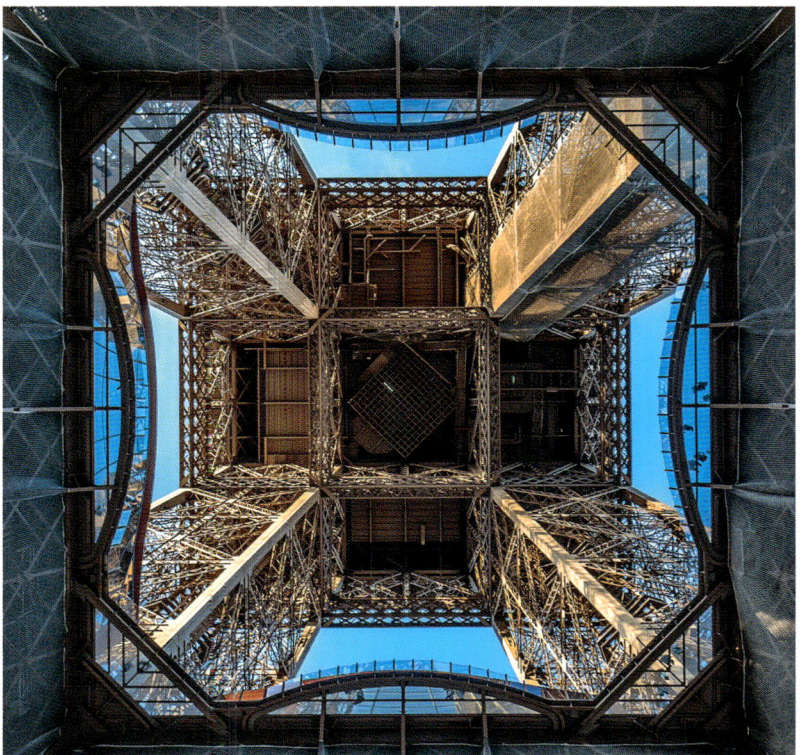

A tower not universally popular at its debut

"A dizzyingly ridiculous tower, dominating Paris like a gigantic factory chimney, crushing, with it barbaric mass, Notre-Dame, Sainte- Chapelle, the Tour Saint-Jacques, the Louvre, the dome of the Invalides, the Arc de Triomphe, all our monuments are humiliated, all our architecture dwarfed, made invisible by this stupefying dream. And for twenty years we shall see spreading across the whole city—a city shimmering with the genius of so many centuries—spreading like an ink stain, the odious shadow of this odious column of bolted metal." That was the verdict of a group of artists—including Guy de Maupassant, Alexandre Dumas, Charles Gounod, Charles Garnier—published in *Le Temps* on February 14, 1887 on the project of the tower not yet called Eiffel.

The bust of Gustave Eiffel, at the foot of the tower.

Champ-de-Mars

7th ARRONDISSEMENT

The Champ-de-Mars was initially laid out as a parade ground for the neighboring École Militaire. This school—built during the reign of Louis XV by Ange-Jacques Gabriel, who also designed the Place de la Concorde—was to train young officers: among its pupils, Napoleon Bonaparte was certainly the most famous.

The Revolution made the Champ-de-Mars an annex of the Republique rather than a barracks; it hosted the Fête de la Fédération on July 14, 1790, celebrating the storming of the Bastille and the dawning of a new age. Two years later, it was the site of the Fête de l'Être Suprême, presided over by Maximilien Robespierre. It did not stop during the Directoire or under the Empire: following his coronation in December 1804, it was here that Napoleon distributed eagle insignia to the army. And during the Hundred Days—when Napoleon returned from exile—it was again at the Champ-de-Mars that the Emperor staged his return to power, with all the electoral colleges and constituted bodies sworn in amidst tens of thousands of soldiers. In the second part of the nineteenth century and until 1937, the World's Fairs were housed at the Champ-de-Mars. The 1889 edition was obviously unusual, with the tower that would become the symbol of Paris rising on the banks of the Seine. Since then, every summer, when the lawns aren't occupied by picnickers and neighborhood children, it regularly plays host to events and concerts with tens of thousands of people.

The Champ-de-Mars, World's Fair of 1900.

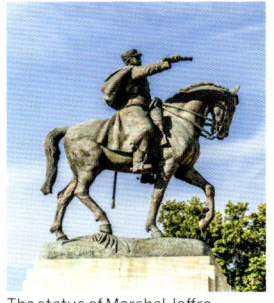

The statue of Marshal Joffre.

École Militaire.

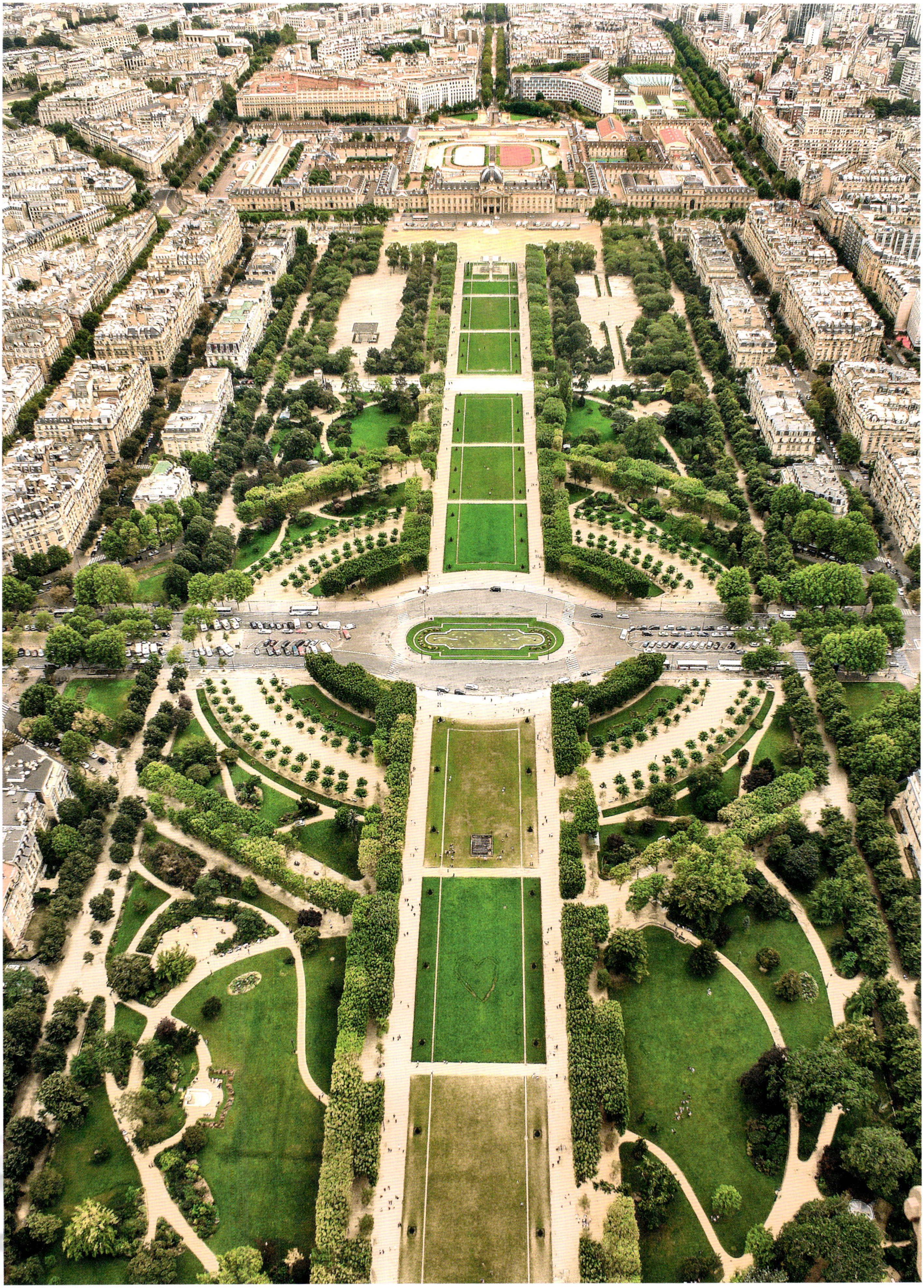

Hôtel des Invalides

ESPLANADE DES INVALIDES, 129 RUE DE GRENELLE (7th)

The Hôtel des Invalides was the brainchild of Louis XIV, eager to offer the wounded and old soldiers of his armies an institution to house them. In 1674, the hotel received its first residents; they would soon be almost seven thousand. Giving onto a vast esplanade, the beautiful, noble facade designed by Libéral Bruant unfolds over nearly two hundred meters; its monumental porch, decorated with a bas-relief of Louis XIV on horseback, in Roman costume gives access to the courtyard. It is another national hero, the bronze of Napoleon I in the uniform of the Chasseurs à Cheval de la Garde Impériale, who wears the stern countenance of the regiment. But it is under the dome that imperial memory rests. On December 15, 1840, the ashes of Napoleon, who had died in exile on Sainte-Hélène almost twenty years before, took the form of a state funeral. However, it would take two decades for the red quartzite crypt and tomb for the imperial remains to be completed.

The Cathedral of Saint-Louis des Invalides has two functions. The dome—the most remarkable ever built in France—crowns the royal chapel. This could have been inspired by Saint Peter's in Rome; the architect Jules Hardouin-Mansart had also planned to complete his work by a large semicircular colonnade comparable to that of the Vatican Basilica. The church under the dome, designed for the exclusive use of Louis XIV, is separated by a glass partition from the nave of the so-called "Soldats" (soldiers) Church, whose gallery is adorned with flags taken from the enemy in all fields of battle.

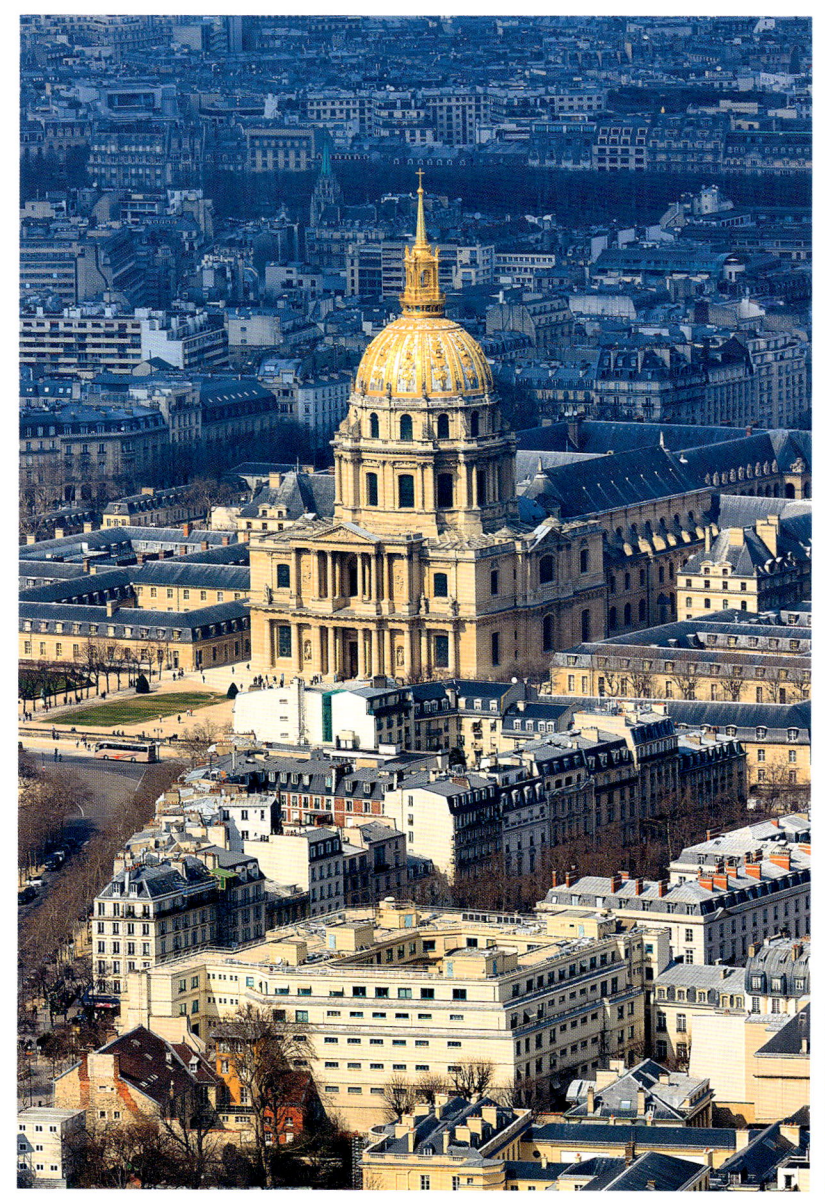

Musée du Quai-Branly

37 QUAI BRANLY (7th)
Officially the Musée des Arts et Civilisations d'Afrique, d'Asie, d'Océanie et des Amériques, the Musée du Quai-Branly, spearheaded by Jacques Chirac during his presidency, was designed by Jean Nouvel and inaugurated in 2006.

The central section of the museum depicts a graceful curve, punctuated with colorful boxes. It is perched on stilts, leaving more space for the garden, designed by renowned landscape architect Gilles Clément.
It is not only on the ground that that nature is at the forefront, as evidenced by the green wall created by Patrick Blanc for the administrative building facing the quay. In the museum's interior, a ramp wraps around, pacing the visit to the 200-meter-long gallery, plunged into darkness and in which cavities housing the permanent collections open, corresponding to the exterior boxes. These collections contain more than four hundred and fifty thousand objects, three thousand five hundred of which are exhibited in spaces dedicated to the four continents covered by the museum. Intersections illustrate the affinities and links among cultures and civilizations that history has relentlessly forged.

The tomb of Napoleon.

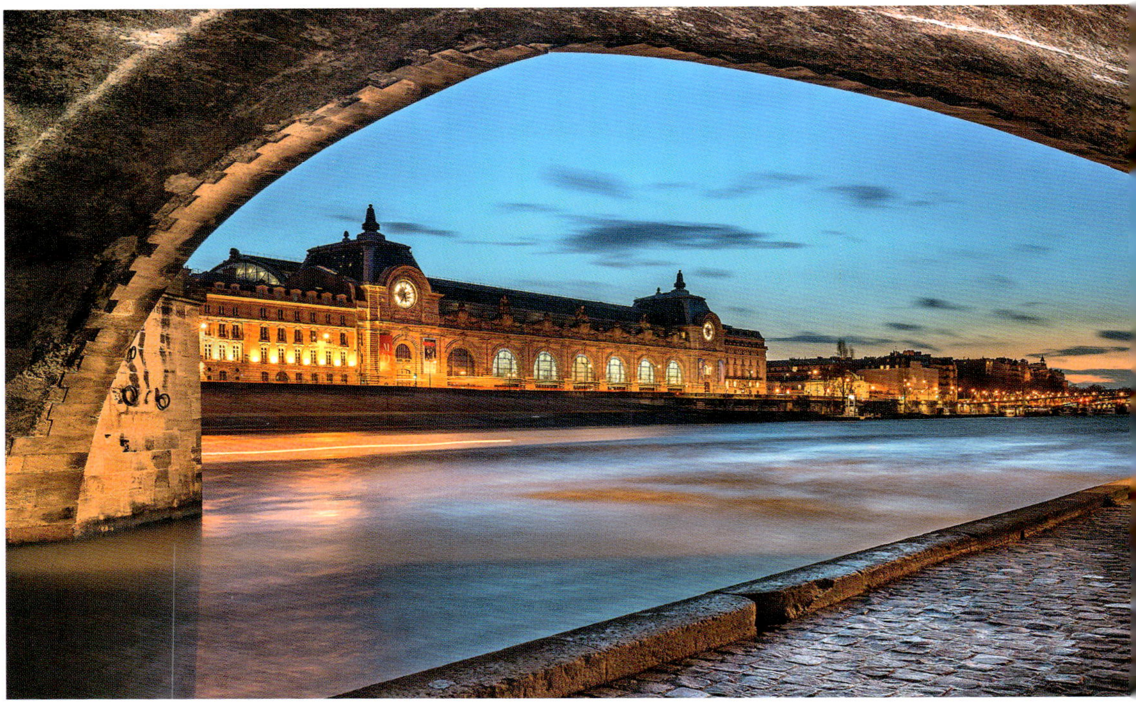

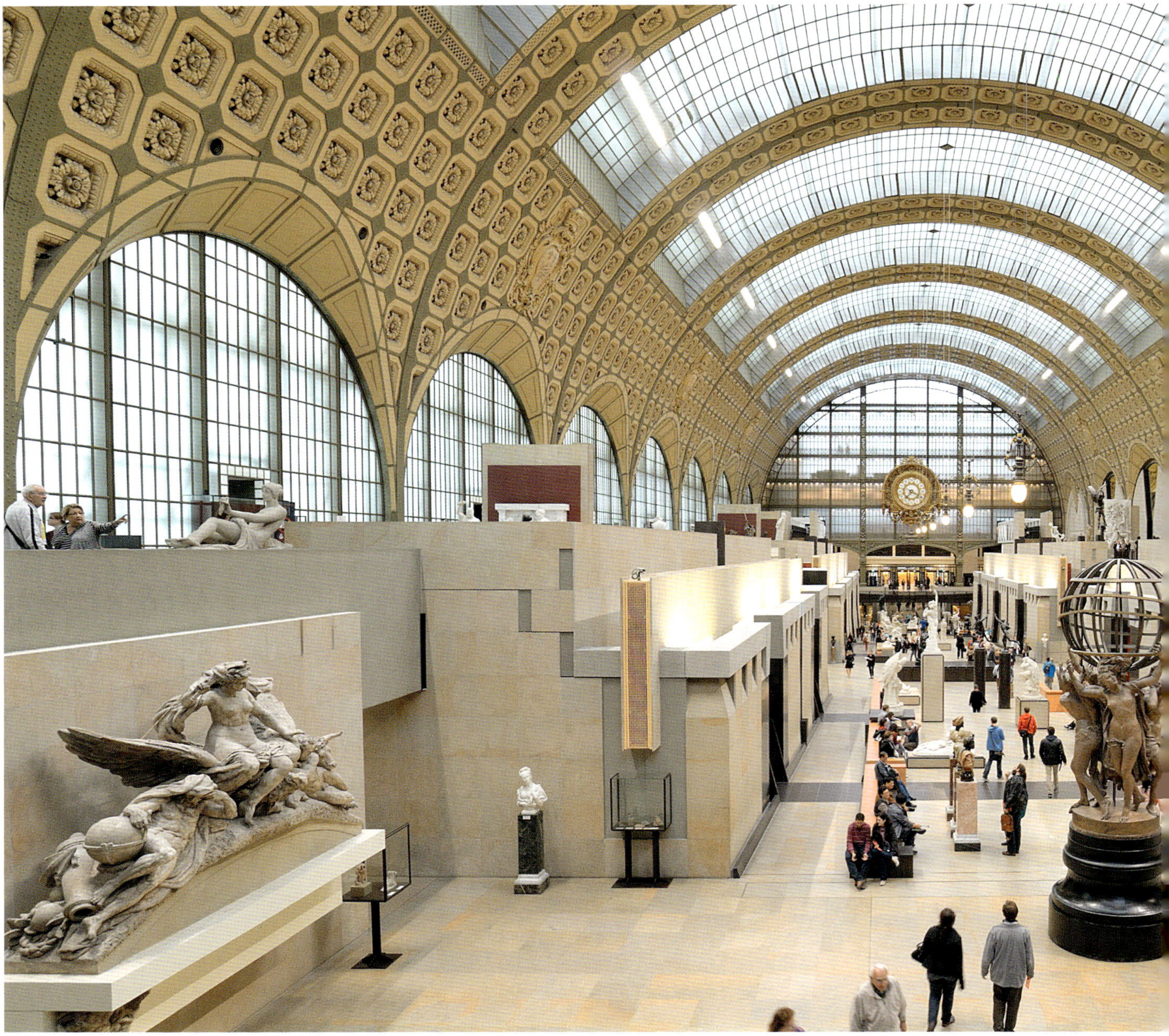

Musée d'Orsay

1 RUE DE LA LÉGION-D'HONNEUR (7th)

In 1900, the building welcomed travelers rather than visitors, as it was then the Gare d'Orsay, the train station serving as the terminus for the Paris-Orléans rail company. Inaugurated for the World's Fair, the Gare d'Orsay was the event's antechamber, offering a luxurious decor banishing steam and soot.

It was a very modern solution but a little impractical, since the trains, still pulled by steam engines, had to be towed from the Austerlitz station by electric motors. This constraint, coupled with platforms too short to accommodate the longer and longer trains, proved fatal for the station. The main line was abandoned in 1939.

A long time was spent searching for a new vocation for the building, before the idea of a museum of nineteenth-century works took shape and the arrangements made. The institution was inaugurated on December 1, 1986. It houses the largest collection of Impressionist works, among which are many canvases by Monet including the *Magpie*, the *Cathedral de Rouen* series, the *Gare Saint-Lazare*, the *Water Lily Pond*, the *Dance at Moulin de la Galette* by Renoir, views around Pontoise and the *Port-Marly* by Pissarro. Manet is present with *Olympia* and *Luncheon on the Grass*, Degas with his dancers, racehorses, *Women Ironing*, Van Gogh with his self-portrait, Courbet with *Origin of the World* and the Artist's Studio. Besides these giants of creation, many other artistic trends—Academism, Symbolism,

Tethered Elephant, by Emmanuel Fremiet.

The statues representing the six continents created for the 1878 World's Fair.

Realism, Orientalism, Fauvism—that emerged in the second half of the nineteenth century are represented. Sculpture has not been overlooked, with Carpeaux to Pompon, Rodin, Bourdelle, Maillol, and more.

Dance at the Moulin de la Galette, by Auguste Renoir, 1876.

Rooftops in the Snow (Snow Effect), by Gustave Caillebotte, 1878.

The Foyer of the Opera at Rue Le Peletier, by Edgar Degas, 1872.

Berthe Morisot with a Bouquet, by Édouard Manet, 1872.

Starry Night, by Vincent van Gogh, 1888.

Poppy Field, by Claude Monet, 1873.

Musée Rodin

79 RUE DE VARENNE (7th)

The museum is housed in the Hôtel Biron, an eighteenth-century mansion. It is not named after its first owner, but the one that enlarged and redeveloped the gardens. From the early twentieth century, after passing through different hands, the Hôtel Biron took in tenants. Among these were many artists, including Jean Cocteau, Henri Matisse and, in 1908, Auguste Rodin, who took over the entire building from 1911. After the sculptor's death, the building was transformed into a museum for his work, which he donated in full to the state. Thus here we can admire his famous pieces, such as the *Thinker*, the *Burghers of Calai*s, the *Kiss*… but as well, many casts, drawings and paintings by Van Gogh, Monet, Renoir and Sargent from the master's collection. A room is dedicated to sculptor Camille Claudel, Rodin's muse and collaborator, with whom he shared a passionate affair.

The Gates of Hell, 1880–90.

The Thinker, 1903, in the garden near the entrance.

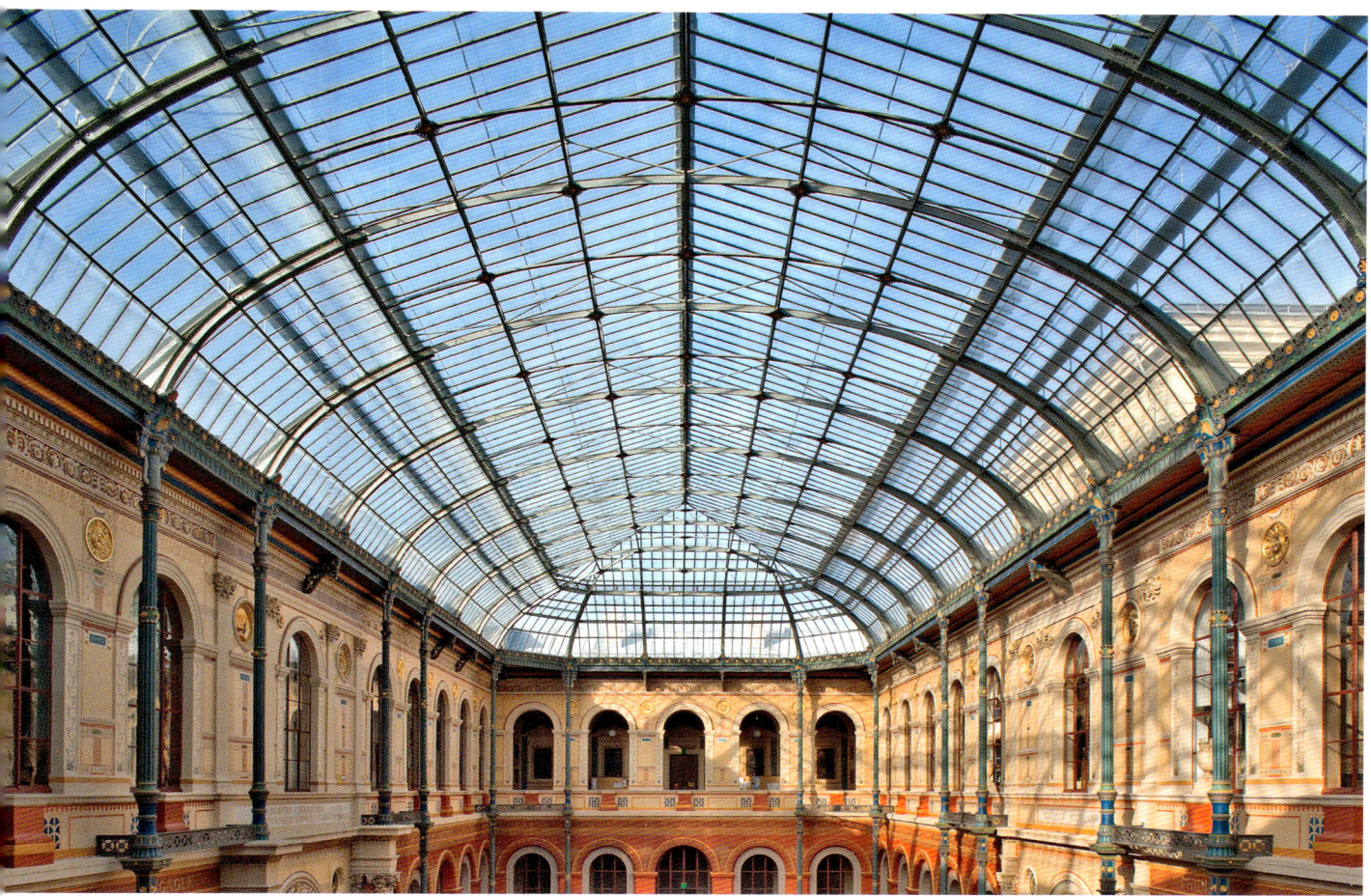

The atrium, Palais des Études.

École des Beaux-Arts

14 RUE BONAPARTE (6th)

The national art school was established in the former convent of the Petits-Augustins, whose chapel remains. During the tumultuous times of the Revolution, Alexandre Lenoir opened the museum of French monuments, displaying statues and architectural elements from religious institutions and noble houses, which would have been destroyed or dispersed without his action. In the early nineteenth century, the site was allocated to the fine arts; a vast Palais des Études was developed along with the main courtyard and the charming Cour du Mûrier from the former convent's cloister. Fragments of various architectures—vestiges of collections gathered by Lenoir—were integrated into the whole.

Cour du Mûrier.

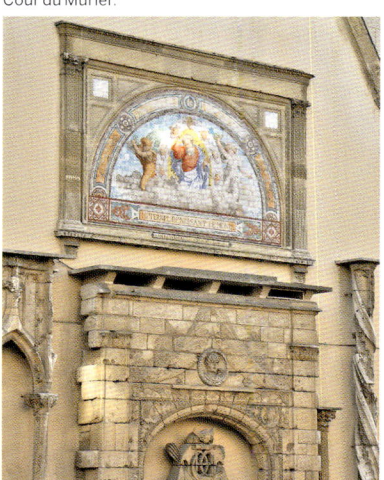

Decorations from the destroyed Hôtel de la Trémoille, reinstalled in the Cour des Beaux-Arts.

Palais des Études.

Institut de France

23 QUAI DE CONTI (6th)

Housing five national academies, of which the most famous is the Académie Française, the institute resides in the former Collège des Quatre-Nations, whose building Cardinal Mazarin expressed a desire for in his will and for which he left part of his immense fortune. It was the architect to the king, Louis Le Vau, who designed the building, whose dome crowns the chapel which was to be the site of the Cardinal's tomb.
This chapel was transformed into a majestic hall, the Salle des Séances and Napoleon offered the site to the institute, and the illustrious academicians have not left since 1805.

The institute's library.

Hôtel de la Monnaie
11 QUAI DE CONTI (6th)

A wonderful example of classical architecture, the hotel was built between 1771 and 1776 to house the Monnaie de Paris, the nation's mint, striking medals and coins, employing almost two thousand workers on the site in the nineteenth century. In 1973, monetary production was transferred to Pessac, in the Gironde region. But special models and medals are still made in Paris, in workshops now visible to the public. Besides revealing the mint's historical collections, contemporary art has been added to the offer, with special exhibitions organized throughout the year. Gastronomy has not been forgotten, with three-starred chef Guy Savoy opening a restaurant in the Hôtel de la Monnaie, overlooking the Seine, the Pont Neuf and the Louvre.

Pont des Arts
1st AND 6th ARRONDISSEMENTS

Inaugurated in 1804, the Pont des Arts was the first steel structure crossing the Seine. Weakened by repeated heavy shocks against its pillars, the bridge finally collapsed in 1979. It was replaced in 1984 by the bridge we know today, which is practically identical to the original, except for the reduced number of arches, matching those of the Pont Neuf to facilitate navigation. During the first decade of the twenty-first century, a wave of "love locks" swept across the bridge, with visitors to the city padlocking their protestations of undying love to the bridge and throwing the key into the river. The heavy weight of these locks meant sections of the bridge gave way and in the summer of 2015 the council removed them, with the locks unfortunately beginning to reappear nearby.

Saint-Germain-des-Prés

PLACE SAINT-GERMAIN-DES-PRÉS (6th)

Place Furstemberg.

The Fontaine de Neptune, Rue du Cherche-Midi.

Inner courtyard, Rue du Cherche-Midi.

Over time, the abbey of Saint-Germain-des-Prés, founded in the middle of the sixth century, sparked the development of a town whose main street was the Rue du Four. The church itself was completely rebuilt around the year 1000 and the nave and most of the bell tower date from this period.

The abbey's holdings were mostly eroded by urbanization in the seventeenth century, before its being declared national property during the Revolution prevented its dismantling. The Rues de l'Abbaye and Bonaparte crossed the estate in the early nineteenth century, opening two major Haussmannian routes, the Rue de Rennes and the Boulevard Saint-Germain, which still jostle the neighborhood. In this site of crossing, an intellectual center flourished around the large university, the majority of the country's publishing houses, literary cafes, prestigious bookstores and art galleries, without forgetting, of course, the cellars, where Juliette Gréco, Boris Vian, Anne-Marie Cazalis and many others congregated, in the golden postwar age, when jazz and existentialism inflamed the Saint Germain nights.

THÉÂTRE DE L'ODÉON

The Théâtre de l'Odéon is the result of subdivision of the Hôtel de Condé's garden in 1779. Five streets are the openings that lead to a site with a semicircular theater, which was the first theater *à l'italienne* in Paris. The building, which is home to the Comédie-Française troop, was inaugurated by Marie-Antoinette in April 1782. Victim of two fires in the early nineteenth century, the theater was rebuilt in 1819 and modified several times. Today it is called the Théâtre de l'Europe and favors a contemporary repertoire transcending borders.

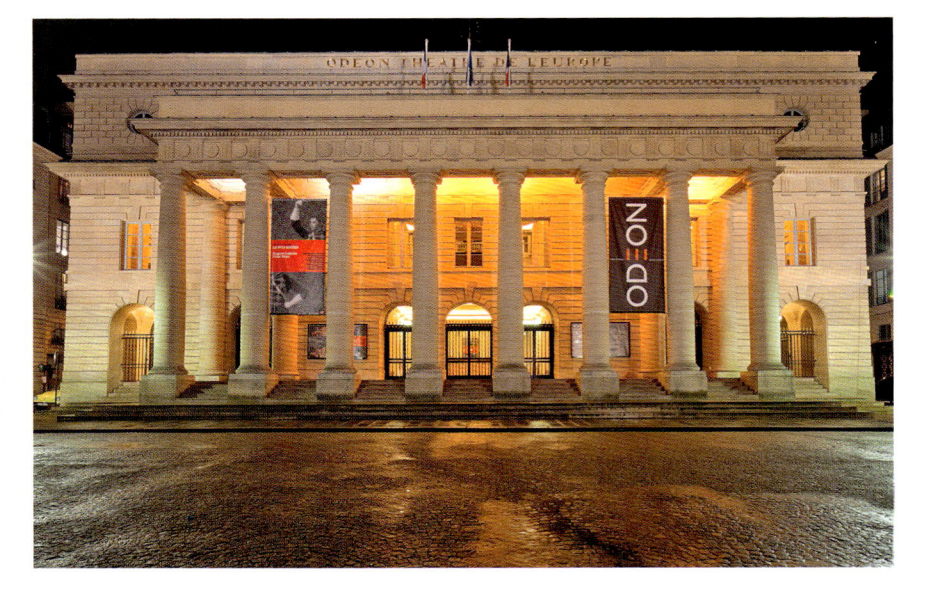

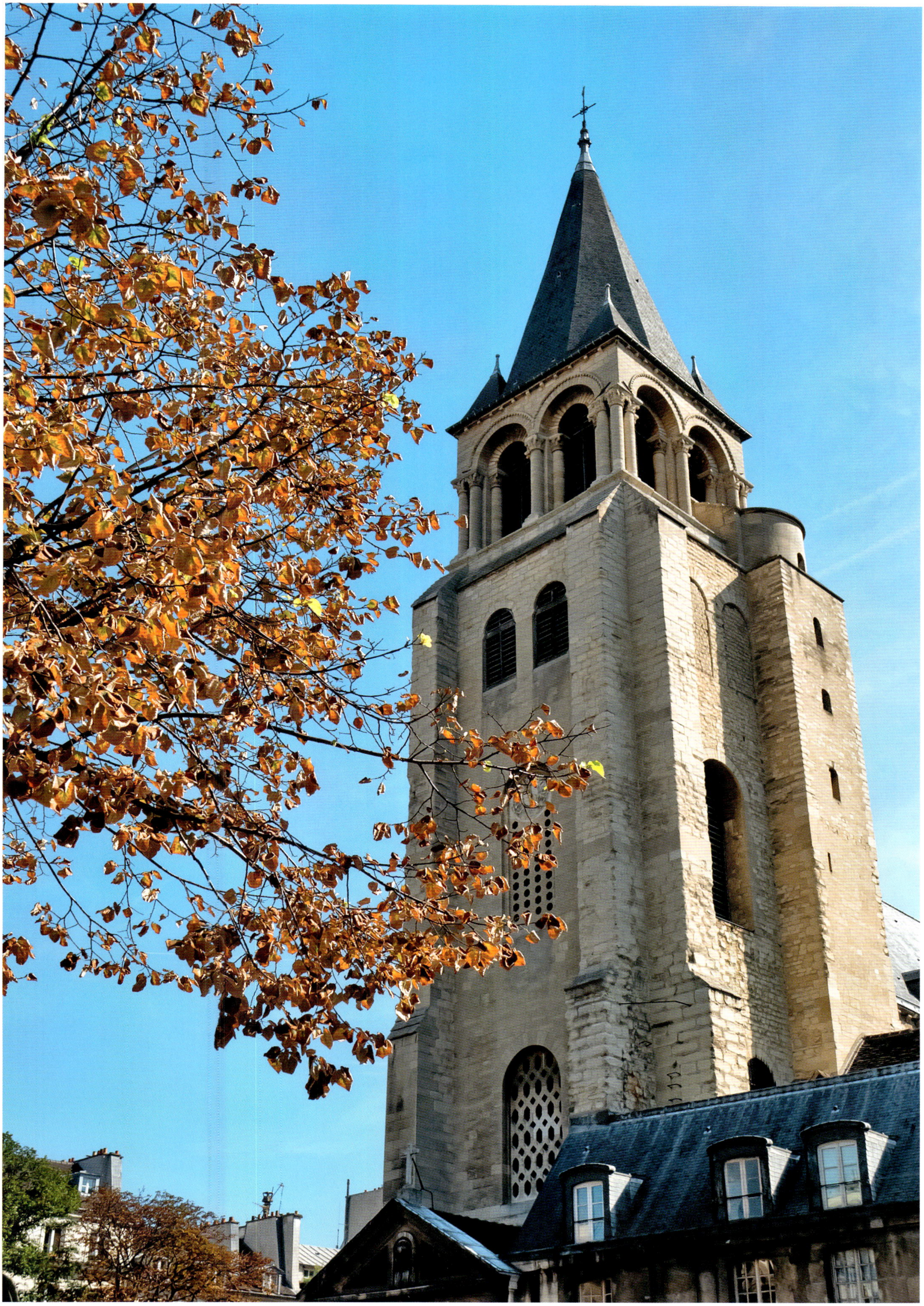

Saint-Sulpice

PLACE SAINT-SULPICE (6th)

This church—one of the largest in Paris—was built over another older, smaller church, which serves as the crypt of the current building. The work for Saint-Sulpice began in the middle of the seventeenth century, and was long interrupted before being finalized in the 1780s. The Revolution stalled the work, leaving the south tower quite narrow, whereas it should have been the exact counterpart to its colleague. Transformed into a Temple of Reason during the Terror, then a warehouse, the church hosted the first optic telegraph experiments in 1798. The south tower was the starting point of a line running relay to relay to Lyon, while the north tower hosted the line running to Strasbourg. Restored as a place of worship, Saint-Sulpice was decorated in the nineteenth century. Three different painters worked there, including Eugène Delacroix in the Chapel of the Holy Angels. In the south transept, the gnomon installed in 1744 remains. This instrument allows, thanks to a copper line embedded in the floor, set to the meridian, the reading of the solar hour, and to determine, above all, the precise March equinox, which governs the dates for Easter.

Notre-Dame-du-Val-de-Grâce

1 PLACE ALPHONSE-LAVERAN (5th)

The Val-de-Grâce church is the result of a vow by the queen, Anne of Austria, wife of Louis XIII, in thanks to God for having given them a son (the future Louis XIV) when the situation seemed hopeless. Architect François Mansart was commissioned, but then sacked after having sunk the entire budget in the consolidation of a single underground mine, in the galleries of the old quarry. After the death of his successor, Jacques Lemercier, Pierre Le Muet and Gabriel Le Duc took over the project. The building was finished in 1665, with its magnificent baroque facade facing Rue Saint-Jacques. The dome, which recalls that of Saint Peter's in Rome, is the highest in Paris after those of the Panthéon and of the Invalides. Inside is housed a spectacular canopy with twisted columns, evocative of Bernini's in the Vatican.

The canopy, by Gabriel Le Duc and the *Altar of the Nativity*, by Michel Anguier.

The Palais and the Jardin du Luxembourg

RUE DE VAUGIRARD (6th)

One of the queens of France who surround the terrace.

After the assassination of her husband, Henri IV, Marie de Médicis was reluctant to reside in the Louvre. Thus in 1615 she acquired the Hôtel de Luxembourg and its neighboring land, and commissioned architect Salomon de Brosse to build a large house, possibly inspired by the Palazzo Pitti in Florence, where the sovereign had spent her childhood. The greatest painters, the most skilled cabinetmakers and the best upholsterers took around a decade to complete its sumptuous interiors. The queen settled in her palace in 1625, but could only enjoy it for a few years before being forced into exile for opposing the all-powerful minister Cardinal Richelieu and her own son, Louis XIII.

The palace has not lost its quality of an aristocratic residence: it was here that Madame de Maintenon raised the children Louis XIV had with his mistress, Madame de Montespan. Later, Louis XVI gifted the property to his brother, the Comte de Provence. During the Revolution, the palace went through several different lives, including as a prison, where notable detainees included Camille Desmoulins, Georges Danton, Joséphine de Beauharnais, the painter Jacques-Louis David, before becoming the seat of the Directoire, in 1795, then under the Empire that of the Senate. The Senate is master of the palace, but the gardens are also held to be the most beautiful in Paris. Expanded with the addition of neighboring land belonging to the Carthusian Order, which was declared national property during the Revolution, the gardens found enough space to move towards the Observatory, as Marie de Médicis had wanted.

Under the First and Second Empires, the openings of the alleys of the Observatory, the Rues de Vaugirard and Auguste-Comte were worked into the garden, forming its current configuration. A wonderful refuge in the heart of the city, Luxembourg is now converted, at the first rays of the sun, into a joyful annex to the neighborhood's universities and high schools.

The Medici Fountain.

Herd of Deer, by Arthur-Jacques Le Duc.

The semicircle of the Senate.

Montparnasse

6th, 14th AND 15th ARRONDISSEMENTS

Montparnasse, specifically the Vavin crossroads, the lyrical soul of the Roaring Twenties, did not hesitate to say that it was the "center of the world." Beyond its excess, the aphorism held a certain reality, when painters, sculptors, writers and photographers from everywhere converged there over two or three decades.

Here, squalid studios crossed with the terraces of grand cafés. Chaim Soutine, Amedeo Modigliani, Pablo Picasso, Georges Braque, Henri Matisse, Tsuguharu Foujita, Ossip Zadkine, Guillaume Apollinaire, Constantin Brancusi, Jean Cocteau and Jacques Prévert … without forgetting the great Americans of the Lost Generation: Ernest Hemingway, F. Scott Fitzgerald, John Dos Passos, Ezra Pound, Man Ray, and later Henry Miller. This effervescence lingers in some of these studios and cafés that are forever associated with Montparnasse … and the legend of a golden age.

At the corner of Rue de la Gaîté and Boulevard Edgar-Quinet.

Rue Notre-Dame-des-Champs.

Tour Montparnasse.

An Art Deco building designed by Henri Sauvage, Rue Vavin.

Musée Zadkine.

Musée Bourdelle.

La Coupole.

La Closerie des Lilas.

La Rotonde.

The Catacombs

PLACE DENFERT-ROCHEREAU (14th)

The collapse of a mass grave in the Cimetière des Innocents into a cellar on the Rue de la Lingerie, and more generally, the congestion of Parisian cemeteries in the last quarter of the eighteenth century, led to the decision to transfer their contents to the former quarries called "Tombe-Issoire"(now in the 14th arrondissement). The unused galleries were arranged to receive the bones from what became the Ossuaire Général de la Ville de Paris. Consecrated in April 1786, they were gradually filled with bones from the Innocents, and then from each of the Parisian cemeteries as they were closed. The remains of some six million Parisians found themselves in the galleries running between the Rues Hallé and Rémy-Dumoncel. Neatly stacked in endless rows of skulls and tibias, the bones hold a macabre aesthetic, conducive to various devotions that have fascinated many generations of visitors. The Catacombs now attract hundreds of thousands of people each year.

OSSEMENTS DU
CIMETIERE DES
INNOCENTS
DÉPOSÉS LE
2 JUILLET 1809

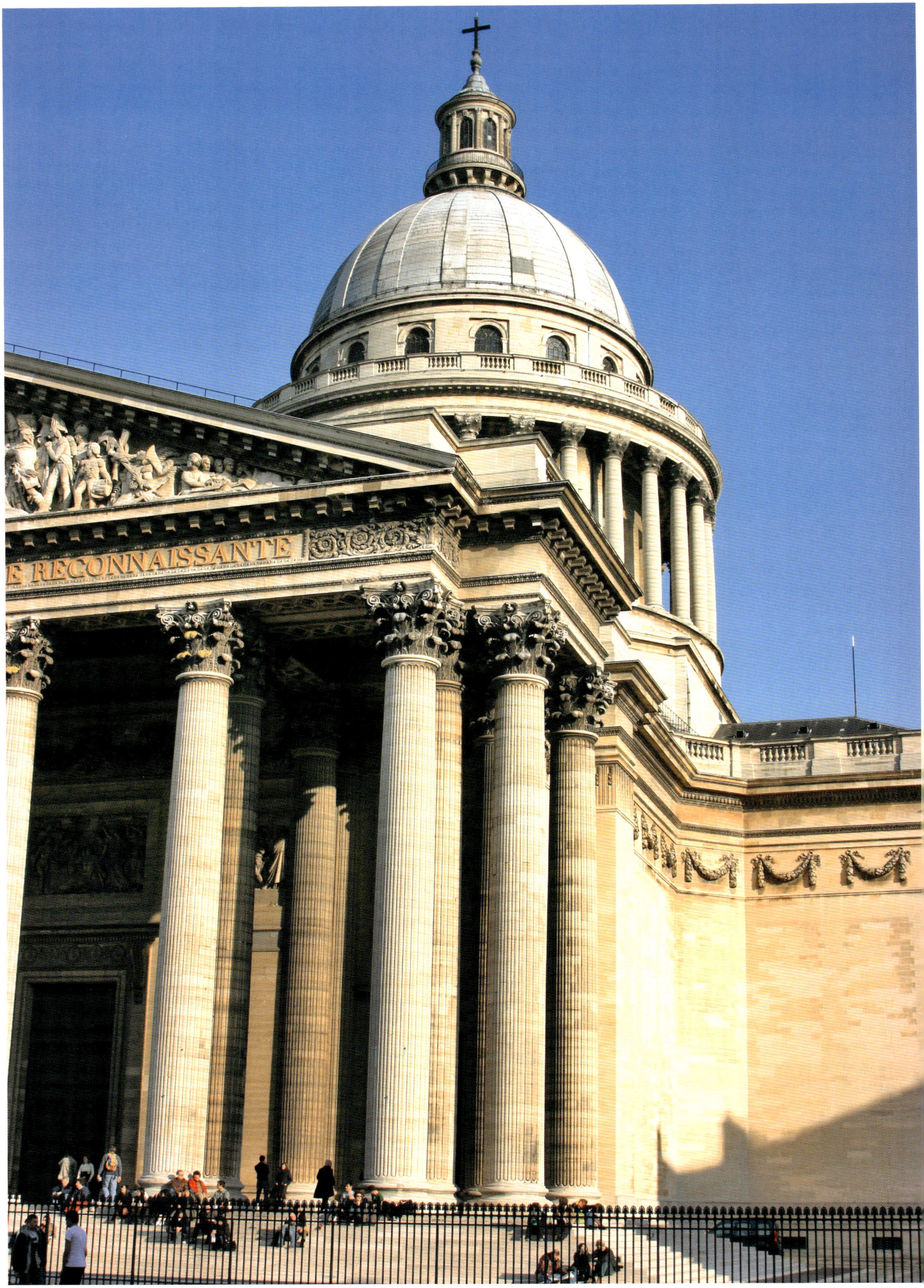
E RECONNAISSANTE

The Panthéon
PLACE DU PANTHÉON (5th)

Nearby the Jardin du Luxembourg, since the Revolution the Panthéon has acted as a temple to great men (with three women for "good" measure). Here lie Voltaire, Jean-Jacques Rousseau, Victor Hugo, Émile Zola, Jean Jaurès, Jean Moulin, and Pierre and Marie Curie. In May 2015, the ashes of four major figures of the Resistance—Geneviève de Gaulle-Anthonioz, Germaine Tillion, Pierre Brossolette and Jean Zay—were transferred there. The original intention was not, however, to build a secular, republican necropolis; Louis XV commissioned architect Jacques-Germain Soufflot to erect a building dedicated to Saint Geneviève. Works were completed in 1790, twenty-five years after the first stones were laid. After some renovations—including the obstruction of windows to plunge the interiors into semi-darkness—in 1791, the church was transformed into a mausoleum. It was returned to a house of worship twice, first under the Empire and then the Second Empire, and definitively took on its current role in 1885, on the occasion of the state funeral for Victor Hugo. The religious decor was removed, while the epigraph "Aux grands hommes, la patrie reconnaissante" [To the great men from the grateful homeland] found its place on the building's pediment.

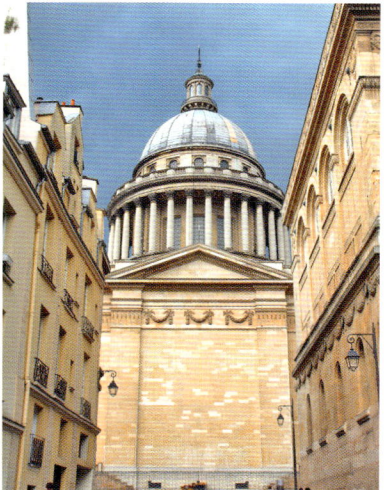

Saint-Étienne-du-Mont
PLACE SAINTE-GENEVIÈVE (5th)

Built between 1492 and 1626, the church mixes, thanks to the long duration of its construction, gothic, Renaissance and baroque styles. It is famous for its rood screen, which crosses the nave from one side to the other, made even more remarkable as it is unique to Paris. Moreover, Saint-Étienne houses the shrine of Geneviève, emptied, however of the relics of the saint, which were burned in the Place de Grève during the revolutionary turmoil.

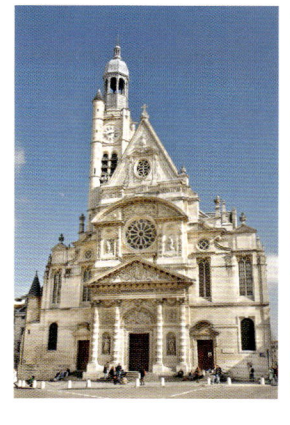

La Sorbonne

PLACE DE LA SORBONNE (5th)

The square in front of the university is something of its extension, with the square's café terraces more frequented than the university's courtyard, which is often deserted. The first university in Paris is also a symbol. Robert de Sorbon founded his college in the Latin Quarter in 1257. In 1622, Richelieu rebuilt the old house and commissioned the architect Jacques Lemercier to design a new chapel. It is the only remnant of the Sorbonne from the seventeenth century, as the university was completely rebuilt at the end of the nineteenth century.

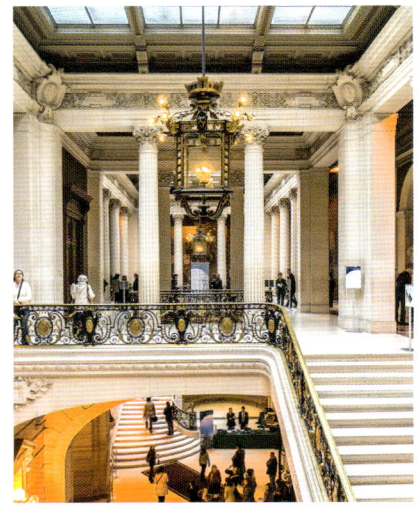

Hôtel de Cluny

6 PLACE PAUL-PAINLEVÉ (5th)

Intended to house the abbots of Cluny, visiting dignitaries and teachers at the college of the same name (which was on the edge of what is now the Place de la Sorbonne), the *hôtel* was built in the late fifteenth century. In 1832, Alexandre Du Sommerard, advisor to the Cour des Comptes took over the Hôtel de Cluny, the only remaining medieval palace in Paris, settling there and installing his collection. On his death, in 1843, the state bought his collection and the *hôtel* to create a proper museum of the baths and the Hôtel de Cluny; its first director was Edmond Du Sommerard, Alexandre's son. Today the site houses the Musée National du Moyen Âge.

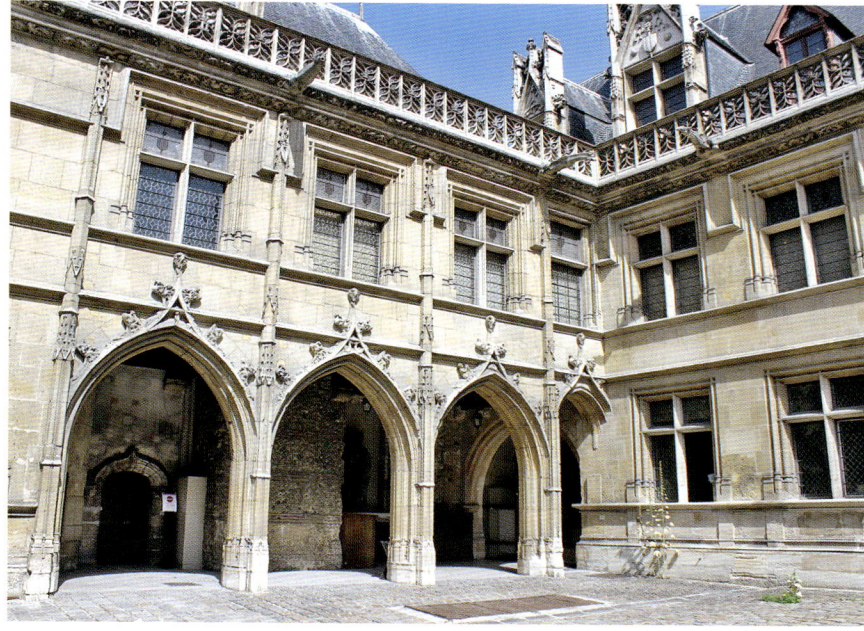

Detail of the tapestry *The Lady and the Unicorn*.

Arènes de Lutèce

49 RUE MONGE (5th)

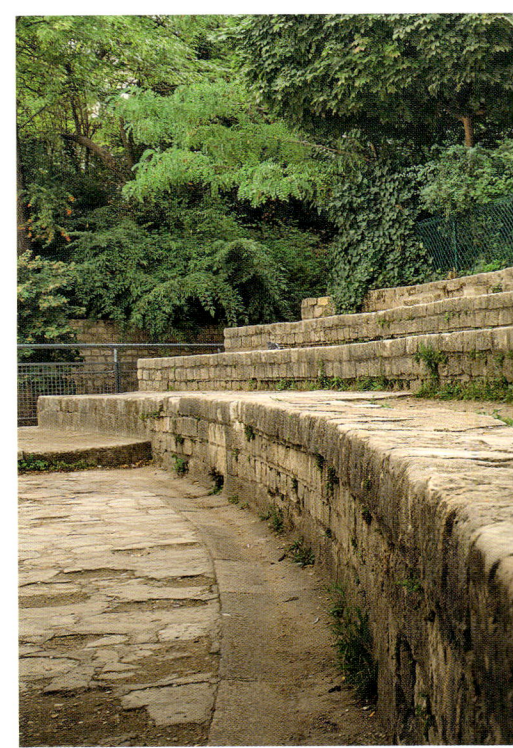

The amphitheater on Rue Monge dates from the first century AD, making it older than the Cluny baths. Seventeen thousand people could sit on its benches to attend the theater or circus games. This rare architectural witness to the Roman city, had completely disappeared from the Parisian landscape, buried in landfill.
It was discovered during the opening of Rue Monge in 1869. Thanks to pressure from Victor Hugo and other intellectuals the arena was saved from destruction for an omnibus depot. A third of the amphitheater was mutilated by the construction of Rue Monge, but the vestiges of the arena were uncovered and restored in 1918.

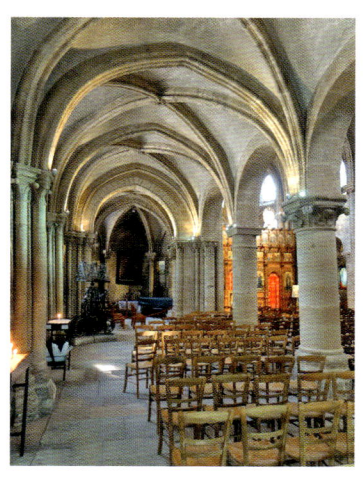

Saint-Julien-le-Pauvre
79 RUE GALANDE (5th)

This sanctuary on the route of the Camino de Santiago is one of the oldest in Paris. Its presence has been attested since the sixth century, although the church was rebuilt many times, notably in 1170. During its busy life, it was fitted with a new facade in the mid-seventeenth century. Turned into a fodder shed during the Revolution, it became relatively obscure, before being vested in 1889 as a Melkite Greek Catholic church.

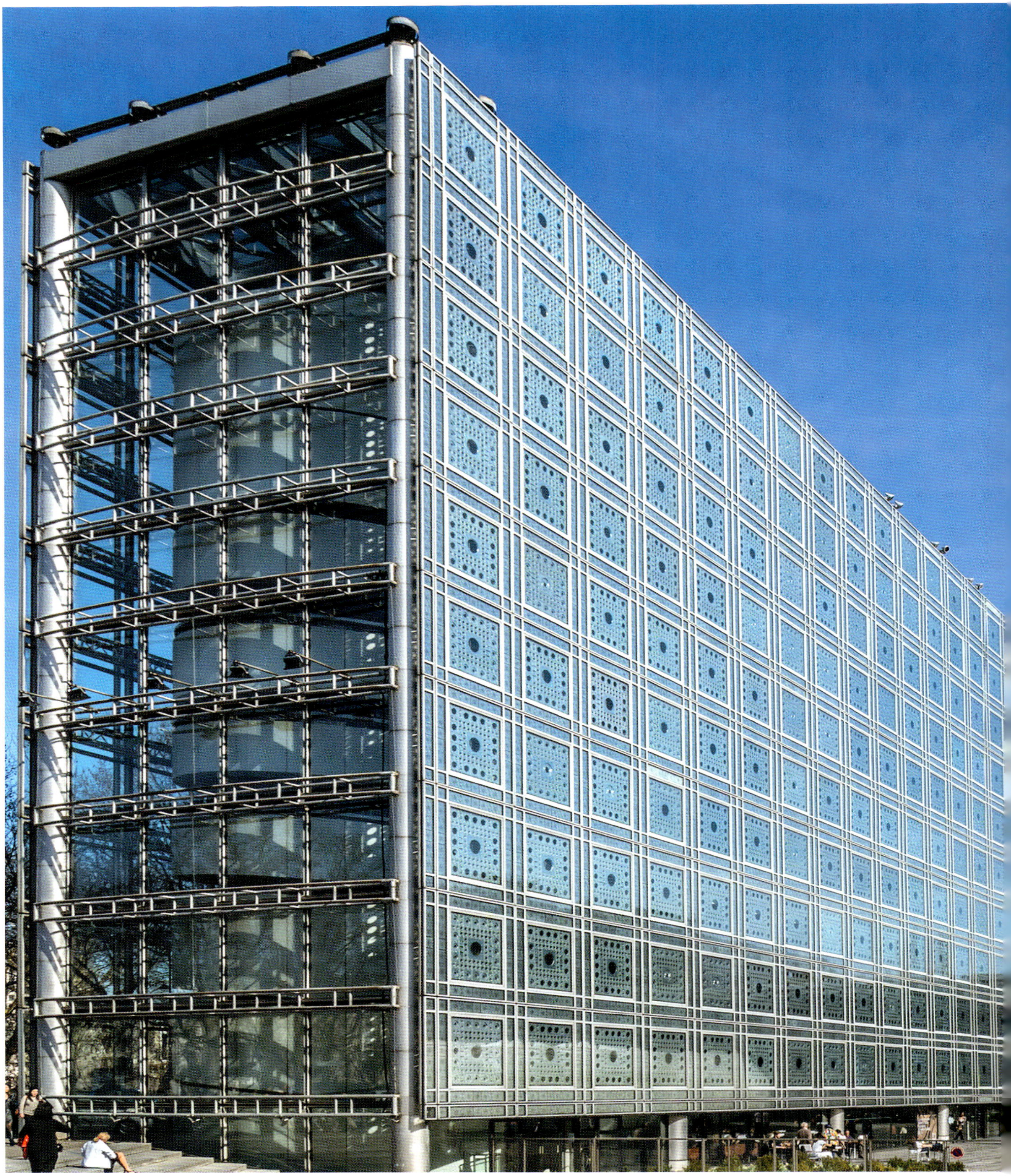

Institut du Monde Arabe

1 RUE DES FOSSÉS-SAINT-BERNARD (5th)

Designed by Jean Nouvel and the Architecture-Studio, the institute was inaugurated in November 1987 by President François Mitterrand. Housing a documentation center, a library, temporary exhibitions and permanent collections, the Institut du Monde Arabe (IMA) was created as a bridge between the Arab and Western cultures. The architects wanted to recapture the spirit of Arab tradition without copying or being a pastiche, but reconciling history and modernity. Thus the building's south facade is made up of thousands of photocell-driven diaphragms regulating the interior lighting according to the external brightness. The entire design inevitably draws comparison to traditional moucharabiehs.
The Quai Saint-Bernard, at the corner of Rue des Fossés-Saint-Bernard, provides a breathtaking view of the institute, whose sections articulate around a space that unifies as it separates. This is in fact true for the entire IMA, remarkable in itself and yet very much part of its environment, extending the lines of the quay onto which it generously opens from its terrace.

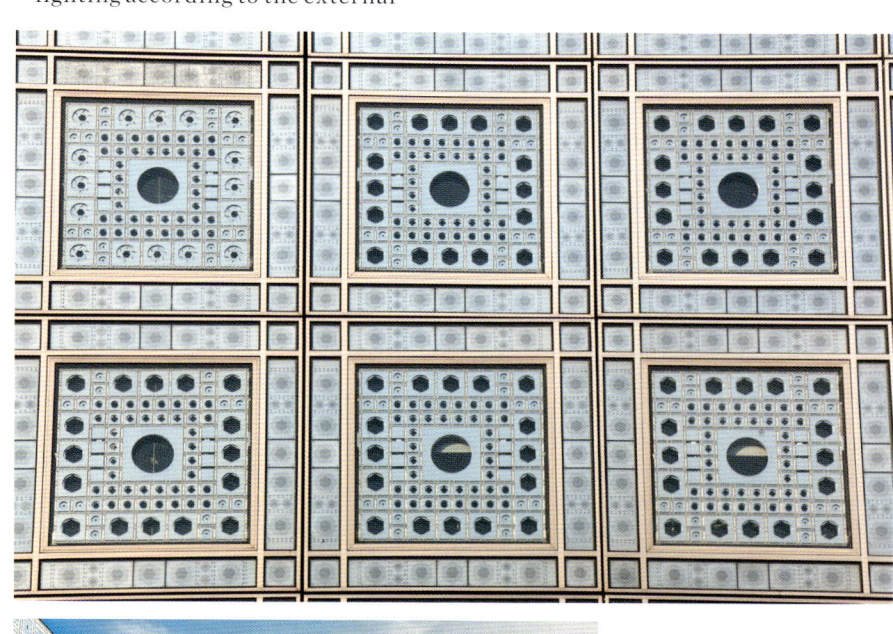

The Jardin des Plantes and the Grande Galerie de l'Évolution

57 RUE CUVIER (5th)

Louis XIII's doctor created the garden in around 1635 to grow medicinal plants and study botany. In the eighteenth century, the naturalist Georges-Louis Leclerc, the Comte de Buffon undertook to transform the apothecary garden into a scholarly center bringing together the best scientific minds of the time. These included Antoine-Laurent de Jussieu who carried in his hat a cedar plant, not from Lebanon, but from London, to plant at the bottom of the Colline du Labyrinthe. The tree is still alive. Besides his botanical school, Buffon took over the king's natural history cabinet so as to gather most of the then-unknown plants in one place. He significantly increased the latter's collections by bringing together all rare and curious pieces he could find, developing it into the largest collection in the world. The cabinet was opened to the public twice a week; the foundations for the museum were laid.

The Revolution took over the institution, while Geoffroy Saint-Hilaire, head of the chair of zoology, set about providing the menagerie. He took part in the 1798 scientific expedition that accompanied Napoleon's Egyptian campaign and grabbed the opportunity to add as many specimens to the collection as possible. Voyages by many other explorers to every continent complemented the museum's rich collections.

Growing continuously over the nineteenth century, the collections went beyond natural history; a mineralogy gallery was built in 1833, another was dedicated to paleontology and the zoology gallery opened in 1889. The latter was completely refurbished in 1994, while simultaneously renewing our view of natural history.

The Buffon Gazebo.

The Grande Galerie de l'Évolution.

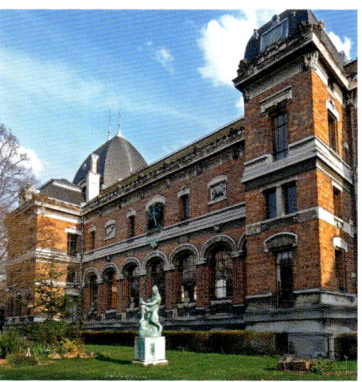

Below, on the mountain

The alpine garden has hundreds of mountain plants from all over the world. Here these plants are grown in a hollow, not at the elevation expected given their origins. They do not seem to mind, thriving on the slopes of their trenched garden.

Tricyrtis formosana.

The paleontology and comparative anatomy gallery.

At the top of the column, the *Spirit of Liberty*.

Place de la Bastille

4th, 11th AND 12th ARRONDISSEMENTS

The Bastille was a fortress protecting the enclosure surrounding Paris, near the royal residence, Hôtel Saint-Pol. It was also a prison: among its illustrious residents were Voltaire and the Marquis de Sade. In July 1789, however, it was little used, and when it was stormed by Parisians it held only seven prisoners.

The Revolution soon razed this symbol of royal despotism; little remains of the Bastille, except a line of cobblestones along the Rue Saint-Antoine indicating its contours. The July Column has stood at the center of the square since 1840, commemorating the revolutionary days of July 1830 and honoring the victims.

With a height of more than fifty meters, it is surmounted by a bronze sculpture, the *Spirit of Liberty*, holding a torch and the broken chains of arbitrary power. Since 1989, the silhouette of the massive Opera-Bastille has blended into the background: the Opéra was inaugurated on July 13 that year, the bicentenary of the Revolution. The nearly three thousand-seat theater offers eastern Paris a "modern and popular" structure that President Mitterand believed would relieve the Palais Garnier.

The Opéra-Bastille.

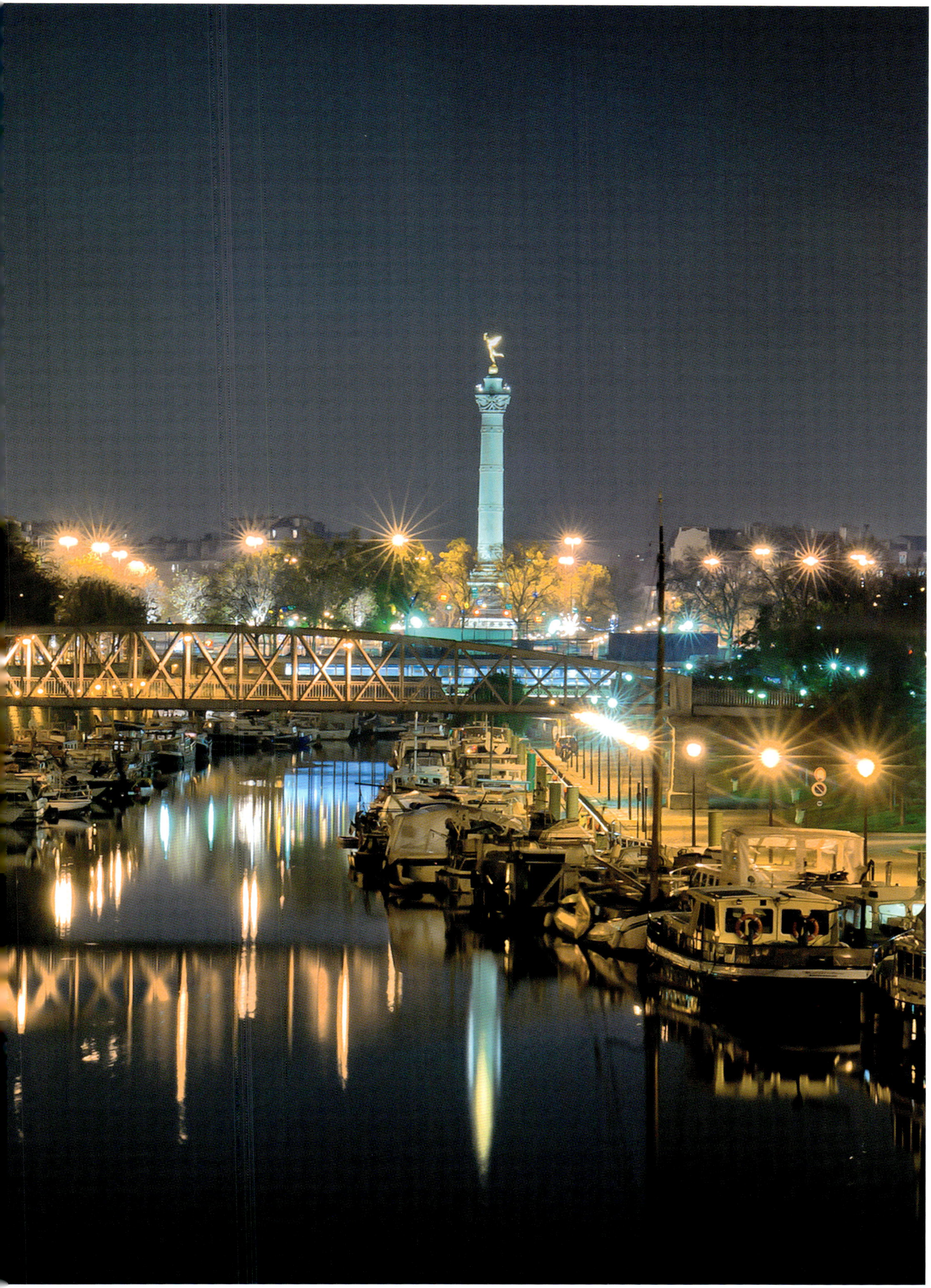

Canal Saint-Martin

10th AND 11th ARRONDISSEMENTS

Napoleon I commissioned the canal to supply Paris with the water it was sorely lacking and with inland waterways offering a shortcut between the meanderings of the Seine. Starting at the Bassin de la Villette, which is itself supplied by the Canal de l'Ourcq, the canal finishes its course at the Port de l'Arsenal, close to the Place de la Bastille. Since 1825, Canal Saint-Martin has never lost a certain "atmosphere," which was captured for posterity by Arletty in Marcel Carné's masterpiece, *Hôtel du Nord*. But there remains little but the facade of this mythic place. Once lined with warehouses and workshops, today the canal is a place to be, as attested by the new generation of cafés, boutiques and restaurants populating the quays.

The Bassin de La Villette and the rotunda built by
Nicolas Ledoux for the Wall of the Farmers-General.

Parc de La Villette and the Cité des Sciences et de l'Industrie

211 AVENUE JEAN-JAURÈS AND 30 AVENUE CORENTIN-CARIOU (19th)

The Cité des Sciences et de l'Industrie was established on the site of Paris's large slaughterhouses. Haussmann created these in the mid-nineteenth century as part of his major works. From 1959, there was a move to more modern facilities; however they proved totally inadequate and uncompetitive. The abattoirs closed in March 1974, and were mostly demolished. On the land left vacant, the Parc de La Villette was established, the largest green space within the city; another of the garden's singularities is that it is not enclosed like its fellow Parisian parks. The Cité des Sciences, whose mission is to popularize scientific culture, found a home in the carcass of the former abattoir's sales hall, begun twenty years earlier. Facing this long building, the visitor is drawn inevitably to the shimmering sphere of the Géode cinema, whose hemispherical screen immerses spectators in the image. Beside the Cité des Sciences is the Grande Halle of the old Haussmannian abattoirs, left in place and converted to a cultural structure. Also nearby the Cité de la Musique, built by Christian de Portzamparc, and the recent Philharmonie de Paris, designed by Jean Nouvel.

One of the twenty-five follies in the park, by Bernard Tschumi.

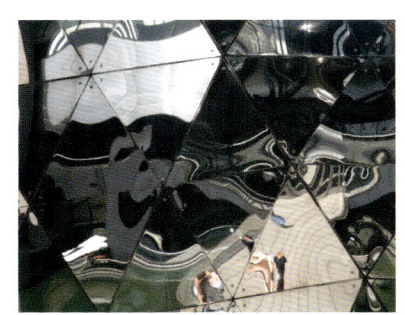

The Géode.

The Cité des Sciences inhabits what were once the sales rooms of the abattoirs.

The Philharmonie de Paris.

The tomb of Victor Noir.

Père-Lachaise cemetery

16 RUE DU REPOS (20ᵗʰ)

The largest Parisian cemetery, Père-Lachaise is also the most visited one, receiving more than three million visitors each year. It was created on Paris's outskirts under the Empire, to replace the old inner-city cemeteries. The architect Brongniart designed an English garden on a former Jesuit estate where one of the notable residents had been Father La Chaise, confessor of Louis XIV.

The cemetery was inaugurated in May 1804, but attracted little attention: by 1806 there were no more than fifty graves. To truly "launch" the site, the municipality transferred the (supposed) remains of the legendary lovers Heloise and Abelard, and of Molière and La Fontaine. This "funeral marketing" worked wonders: by 1830 more than 30,000 graves had flourished in the shady plots. Today there are more than 70,000. Apart from the many famous residents, Père-Lachaise is a historic site. During the last days of the Commune, rebels and troops clashed among the graves. On May 28, 1871, the last survivors were shot in front of the wall later called the "Mur des Fédérés."

Oscar Wilde's grave.

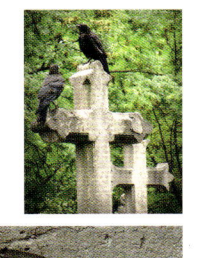

Montmartre

18th ARRONDISSEMENT

The Butte Montmartre is part of Paris, but bears little resemblance to it, with its village allure, winding alleys and stairs. For a long time gypsum was extracted from it subsoil, to be turned into plaster that was widely used in all the capital's construction sites, resulting in the saying that "there is more of Montmartre in Paris than Paris in Montmartre."

The site was originally dedicated to Mercury, under the name Mons Mercuri, before becoming the Mons Martyrium. The legend of Saint Denis relates that he was beheaded at mid-slope of the hill before he picked up his head, washed it in a fountain on Rue Girardon and continued on his way north before falling at the site where, later, the Basilica of Saint-Denis would be built.

The hill has always been a center of spirituality, home to a Benedictine Abbey of Montmartre. This same order planted the vines that covered almost all of the hill's slopes. The village, which had fewer than three hundred houses in the mid-seventeenth century, saw twenty mills take possession of its heights at the same time; milling thus became an important activity. The majority of the mills housed a *guinguette*, a kind of dance hall: the Parisian working classes thronged to them each Sunday to enjoy the fresh air and enjoy the (bad) wine, cheaper than in the city, since it was exempt from the capital's import taxes. Is it for such charms of rustic Monmartre that artists settled in large numbers at the end of the nineteenth and early twentieth centuries? Perhaps, but mostly because there were inexpensive studios. The stairs we climb today were trod by Vincent van Gogh, Renoir, Henri de Toulouse-Lautrec, Amedeo Modigliani, Maurice Utrillo, Jules Pascin, Pierre Bonnard, Pablo Picasso, and more.

Moulin de la Galette.

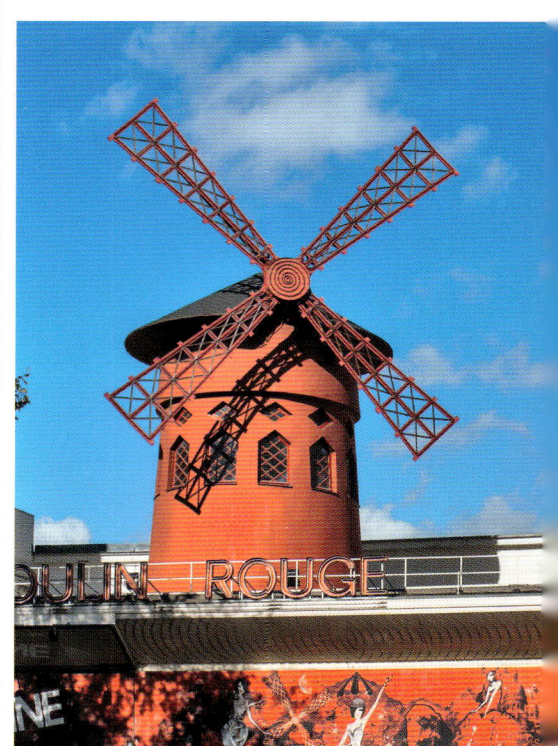

Moulin rouge.

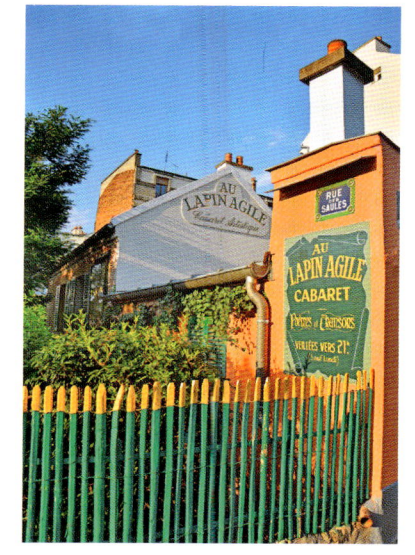

Musée de Montmartre

12 RUE CORTOT (18th)

Au Lapin Agile

Would the place be as famous without it? When the owner asked cartoonist André Gill to make a new sign, the venue was the Cabaret des Assassins: in 1880, Gill created the famous rabbit leaping from a pot, and the cabaret became known as the Lapin Agile. The cabaret became the place for bohemian Montmartre to meet, with regulars including Aristide Bruant, Alphonse Allais, Henri de Toulouse-Lautrec and Georges Courteline, and then in the twentieth century… Pablo Picasso, Pierre Mac Orlan, Roland Dorgelès, André Salmon, Guillaume Apollinaire and Charles Dullin. It was here in 1910, that Dorgelès mounted the hoax of a painting by a donkey, shown at the Salon des Indépendants to mock the vanguard advocating abstraction.

Rue Cortot.

The museum is housed in the oldest house in Monmartre, surrounded by a beautiful garden; it enjoys an incomparable view over the vineyards of the Butte, the Cabaret du Lapin Agile and the rooftops of northern Paris. Here many painters had their studios, including Pierre-Auguste Renoir who rented a room on the ground floor in 1875. Nothing remains, except the studio of Suzanne Valadon and her son, Maurice Utrillo, beautifully restored. The museum's collections evoke the history of the Butte in all its aspects, from the most modest cabarets to the stage of the Moulin Rouge, from the lively theater of the Chat Noir to the Bateau-Lavoir and its creative fever.

The vines of Montmartre, at the foot of the museum.

Sacré-Cœur

PARVIS DU SACRÉ-CŒUR (18th)

Equestrian statue of Joan of Arc.

On top of the hill, the Sacré-Cœur stands in the Parisian sky. The basilica was built over more than forty years, to atone for the lowered national moral following the loss of the Franco-Prussian war and the heartbreak of the Commune in 1871. More than ten million faithful contributed, often modestly, to a national subscription to finance the project.
Sacre-Cœur represents the majority, conservative rural France, manifesting its rejection of revolutionary and minority Paris. But the unstable subsurface of the hill, quarries of old gypsum mines, more or less filled in, imposed foundations other than the purely ideological. Over eighty wells were drilled to pour concrete supports for the building.
Built in the shape of a Greek cross, Sacré-Cœur has four domes, the highest reaching 83 meters. From its outside gallery, the view reaches 50 kilometers in clear weather. The basilica is built from stone from the Château-Landon, which is self-cleaning in the rain, the reason for the building's permanent whiteness. Sacré-Cœur is a site of pilgrimage and a sanctuary of perpetual adoration. The latter takes the form of uninterrupted prayer, day and night since the basilica's consecration in 1916. In visitor numbers, the basilica is the second most popular religious monument in France, behind Notre-Dame.

Place du Tertre

The old center of Montmartre when the area was still a village, the Place du Tertre was home to the first town hall, built at number 3 in 1790, and the restaurant À la Mère Catherine, whose doors have been open since 1793. Drawing on the site's artistic traditions, painters specializing in picturesque views of Paris, or the imitation of great names, have now moved in. Flanked by cartoonists and silhouette cutters, they look for business, sometimes quite insistently, from passing tourists.

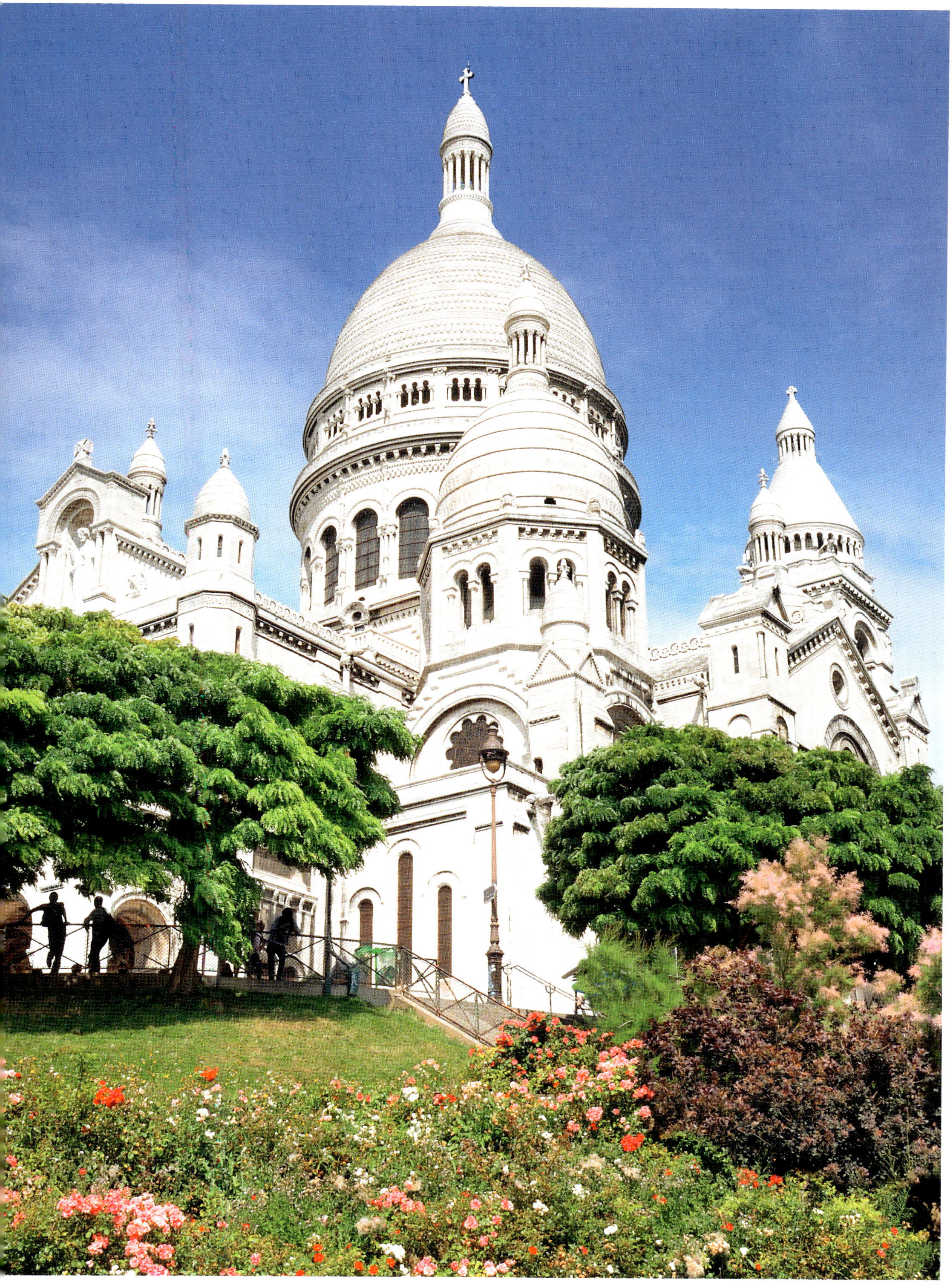

Opéra-Garnier

PLACE DE L'OPÉRA (9th)

Symbol of the Napoleon III style, with its abundance of sculptures, gilt and colors, the Palais de l'Opéra, built by Charles Garnier, was opened in 1875. The theater is one of the largest and vastest in the world, though it seats only around two thousand because of the extensive spaces dedicated to the backstage and rehearsal rooms, space that gavs free reign to the display of pomp and sophistication at imperial events.

Here, more than anywhere else, the show is in the theater as much as on the stage, or rather, it is the Opéra Garnier itself: the sumptuous staircase, all curves and scrolls, marble, onyx, copper and mosaics, designed to see and to be seen in. A huge chandelier weighing nearly eight tons, hung as high as a two-story house, lights the large red-and-gold room, with five boxes. Outside, on either side of the copper dome, are two gilded bronze figures, *Poetry* and *Harmony*. In the center, Apollo brandishes his lyre. Under the loggia and the portico, several sculpted groups animate the facade. Among them, *The Dance* by Jean-Baptiste Carpeaux, which, thanks to its distance from academic conventions, caused a scandal when it was installed. In August 1869, one hothead threw a bottle of ink over these stone women, shouting "smelling of vice and reeking of wine"! Today the work is in the Musée d'Orsay, replaced by a copy on the Opera, not to protect it from new protests, but from the damage of pollution. The construction of the Palais Garnier led to the development of the square that cuts Boulevard des Capucines in two and crosses Avenue de l'Opéra. This had no other purpose except than to allow Napoleon III a quick, safe connection between the Palais des Tuileries, where he lived, and the theater. It did, though, offer a spectacular view on to the Opéra. It is the only avenue in Paris not planted with trees; Charles Garnier strongly opposed Haussmann on this subject, and vigorously fought to keep any foliage from hiding his masterpiece.

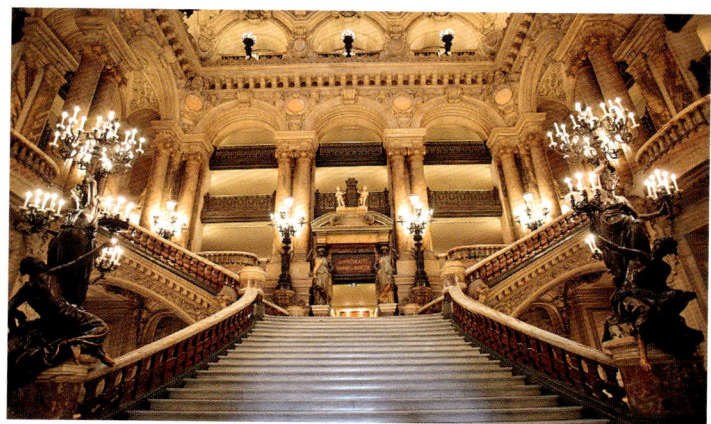

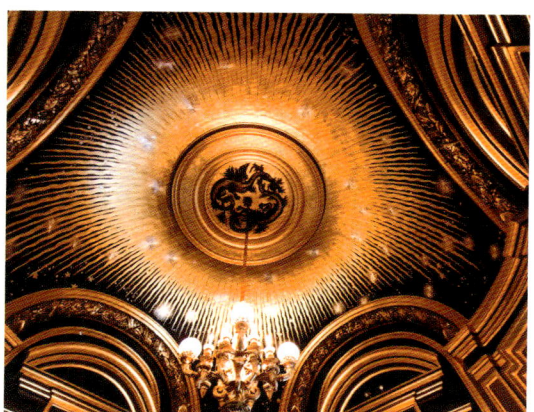

The Salon du Soleil.

A window at Galeries Lafayette.

The Grands Boulevards

2nd, 3rd, 9th, 10th, 11th ARRONDISSEMENTS

The Morris Column, by Jean Béraud, c. 1885.

The BNP headquarters, Boulevard des Italiens.

The Grands Boulevards were built on the old fortifications surrounding Paris. It was Louis XIV who made Paris an open city by destroying the old wall, which was all the more useless since it could not have resisted an artillery attack. A long promenade, planted with a double row of trees, was created; a few temporary huts appeared, as did street performers, at first just a few, but growing in numbers in accord with the increasing visitors to the area.

Subsequently, the edges of the boulevards were subdivided into buildings and sometimes townhouses, while the road was paved and street lighting was installed. A fine clientele crowded the cafés and luxury restaurants around the Opéra, while today's Place de la République, did not disappoint popular opinion as the "boulevard of crime"—thus named because of the liters of blood spilt there every night—for entertainment of course, on the stages of the neighborhood's many theaters. After the golden age of the nineteenth century, the Grands Boulevards' star paled somewhat ... which did not stop Yves Montand singing in 1951, "J'aime flâner sur les grands boulevards / Y a tant de choses, tant de choses/ Tant de choses à voir ..." [I Like to stroll on the boulevards /There are so many things, so many things / So much to see ...] So much to see, like the windows of Galeries Lafayette on Boulevard Haussmann, which is not part of the Grands Boulevards' historical arc, but is associated with it by visitors nevertheless. The first store opened in 1894, on the corner of Rue La Fayette and Rue de la Chaussée-d'Antin. It grew quickly, first taking up the entire building and then a number of its neighbors. The new temple to commerce, wearing a sumptuous cupola and hemmed with scalloped balconies, was inaugurated in October 1912. Each year, more than twenty-five million customers visit this luxuriously decorated flagship!

Musée Grévin

10 BOULEVARD MONTMARTRE (9th)
Since 1882, the Musée Grévin has given a wax face to celebrated figures. Among the oldest effigies is Jean-Paul Marat—the bathtub the Revolutionary's waxen replica sits is the same one in which he was murdered. It was bought for 5,000 gold francs in 1885. The most recent residents include Pope François, singer Édith Piaf and soccer player Zlatan Ibrahimovic.

The Covered Passages

1st, 2nd, 9th AND 10th ARRONDISSEMENTS

Born at the end of the eighteenth century, the Parisian arcades experienced a brief golden age before the immense works of the Second Empire, which began in 1850, sealed their decline. These galleries were built in the heart of a still-medieval Paris, where the streets were not always paved, and lacked both sidewalks and sewers.

Needless to say, these streets did not invite you to stroll, much less window shop. In comparison, wandering through a covered arcade, protected from the weather and the traffic, lit, sometimes heated and often richly decorated, had all the walker could dream of! These covered galleries—"lascivious lanes of commerce," in the words of Walter Benjamin—were ideally placed in proximity to the boulevards, the theaters and the cafés. They seduced through their luxury and their entertainments, and asserted themselves in a fashionable society that liked nothing better than to enjoy its own show.

The urban reform led by Baron Haussmann, with its large avenues and train stations, however, upset the scale of public space, as the department stores changed that of commerce. Many arcades were destroyed; others fell into a sweet slumber, abandoned by the crowds that once thronged there. Around twenty Parisian arcades and their beautiful decor survive, sometimes making antiquated parentheses in the heart of the city.

Passage des Panoramas.

Passage du Grand-Cerf.

Galerie Véro-Dodat.

A store in the Passage des Panoramas.

Galerie Vivienne.

Musée Jacquemart-André

158 BOULEVARD HAUSSMANN (8th)

The mansion was built in 1875 for Édouard André, very rich heir to a lineage of bankers and a great collector, who married Nélie Jacquemart in 1881. The couple traveled widely in Europe and around the Mediterranean, visiting antiquarians, acquiring pieces destined to nourish their exceptional collection of paintings, sculptures and objets d'art from the Renaissance to the eighteenth century. After Nélie's death in 1912, the mansion and collection were bequeathed to the Institut de France to create a museum, which is the one we can visit today. It allows us to discover not only a priceless collection, but also the opulent interiors of a pair of aesthetes with unlimited means.

Léda, by Gustave Moreau, 1869.

Musée Gustave-Moreau
14 RUE DE LA ROCHEFOUCAULD (9th)

The symbolist master, Gustave Moreau, moved into this townhouse—in the residential district dubbed Nouvelle Athènes—in 1852. Here he composed a host of paintings inhabited by a fantasy world all his own. Unicorns, chimeras, griffons and mythological creatures reigned supreme in the studio, which transformed into a museum at the artist's death in 1898. You can visit the apartments decorated by Moreau and his studios on the second and third floors, connected by an elegant spiral staircase.

Musée de la Vie Romantique
16 RUE CHAPTAL (9th)

This house, nestled in a charming garden, was built in 1830. It belonged to the Romantic painter Ary Scheffer, who over thirty years hosted his neighboring artists, musicians and writers of the Nouvelle Athènes and elsewhere. George Sand, Frédéric Chopin, Franz Liszt, Alphonse de Lamartine, Eugène Delacroix, Ernest Renan, etc. wandered along the same uneven pathway that visitors use today. In the green-shuttered house, they discover, souvenirs (jewelry, objects, furniture and more) of George Sand and paintings by Scheffer, who was the drawing teacher of the children of the Duc d'Orléans, who was later the king, Louis-Philippe.

Parc Monceau

35 BOULEVARD DE COURCELLES (8th)

The park is the remnant of a much larger property, once owned by the Duc de Chartres, converted into a "Chinese" garden, that is to say, with winding pathways and "follies"—a pagoda, grottos, pavilions, a labyrinth and mills—transporting the visitor to an exotic elsewhere. All that remains is a modest pyramid and the Naumachie, an oval pool surrounded by a colonnade. At the entrance, on the Boulevard de Courcelles, the rotunda is one of four pavilions that still remain from the forty-seven that architect Nicolas Ledoux had built as barriers against the Farmers General at the end of the Ancien Régime: Prefect Haussmann destroyed this fiscal wall and most of its pavilions. At the same time, the park was converted into a public garden and its periphery subdivided into townhouses.

exceptional collection of seventeenth-century art. It was given to France after his death on the condition that the museum carry the name of his son, Nissim de Camondo, a pilot during the First World War, whose plane was shot down over Alsace. Besides admiring the wonderful collection, visitors can discover the organization and scale of a rich Parisian home of the early twentieth century, from the kitchen to the salon, the bathroom to the library.

The Petit Pont.

The "Naumachie."

The Masonic pyramid.

One of the most spectacular townhouses was built on Avenue Van-Dyck for wealthy chocolatier Émile-Justin Menier. The most remarkable residence that remains, however, is at 63 Rue de Monceau. The Count Moïse de Camondo built this townhouse in 1912, in imitation of the Petit Trianon in Versailles, to house his

The seventeenth-century salon and the kitchen of the Hôtel de Camondo.

The Champs-Élysées

8th ARRONDISSEMENT

The "most beautiful avenue in the world" was first a simple path designed by André Le Nôtre to the west of the Jardins des Tuileries to provide these gardens with a view. At the beginning of the eighteenth century, the avenue was extended until what is now the Place de l'Étoile. It was bordered with stalls and taverns of more or less good repute; it was only under the Directoire and the Empire that the most select establishments chose to open their doors on the Champs-Élysées and it became an elegant promenade. Under Napoleon III, townhouses and prestigious buildings lined its two sides. Subsequently, the world of business and commerce made the avenue its window—automakers, airlines, international banks and cinema chains made it their address. But it is also at moments of major historical importance or sporting victories that the Champs-Élysées comes into its own, becoming the triumphal road of an enthusiastic people.

The twelve avenues radiating from Place Charles-de-Gaulle.

Arc de Triomphe

PLACE CHARLES-DE-GAULLE (8th)

Napoleon commissioned the Arc de Triomphe in 1806, to honor the Great Army, but it wasn't completed until 1836, after the emperor's death. The arch boasts the largest collection of sculptures from the first half of the nineteenth century, with the famous high relief of *La Marseillaise* carved by François Rude and works by Jean-Pierre Cortot, James Pradier, Antoine Etex and the best artists of the period.

The arcades are engraved with the names of the 660 generals involved in the imperial army's battles; those who lost their lives are underlined. Under the arch is the tomb of the Unknown Soldier, an anonymous victim of the Great War. The flame of remembrance is rekindled every evening. It took time for this monument—as for all of them—to become a unique national symbol. In December 1840, the cortege accompanying Napoleon's ashes passed under the Arc. In May 1885, during the state funeral for Victor Hugo, the monument was draped in black and surrounded by more than a million people. But it was on July 14, 1919, on the occasion of the "victory parade," the first following the Great War, that the Arc de Triomphe appeared as the altar of the nation. The Unknown Soldier was buried in 1921, and subsequently, at every important national celebration presidents succeeded one another. Built in the Second Empire, the Place de l'Étoile was designed to magnify the Arc. Haussmann created it to add seven routes to those already existing, to achieve the balanced composition of a twelve-pointed star, while Hittorff designed the townhouses that line the site and give it a unified appearance.

The Departure of the Volunteers of 1792, or *La Marseillaise*, by François Rude.

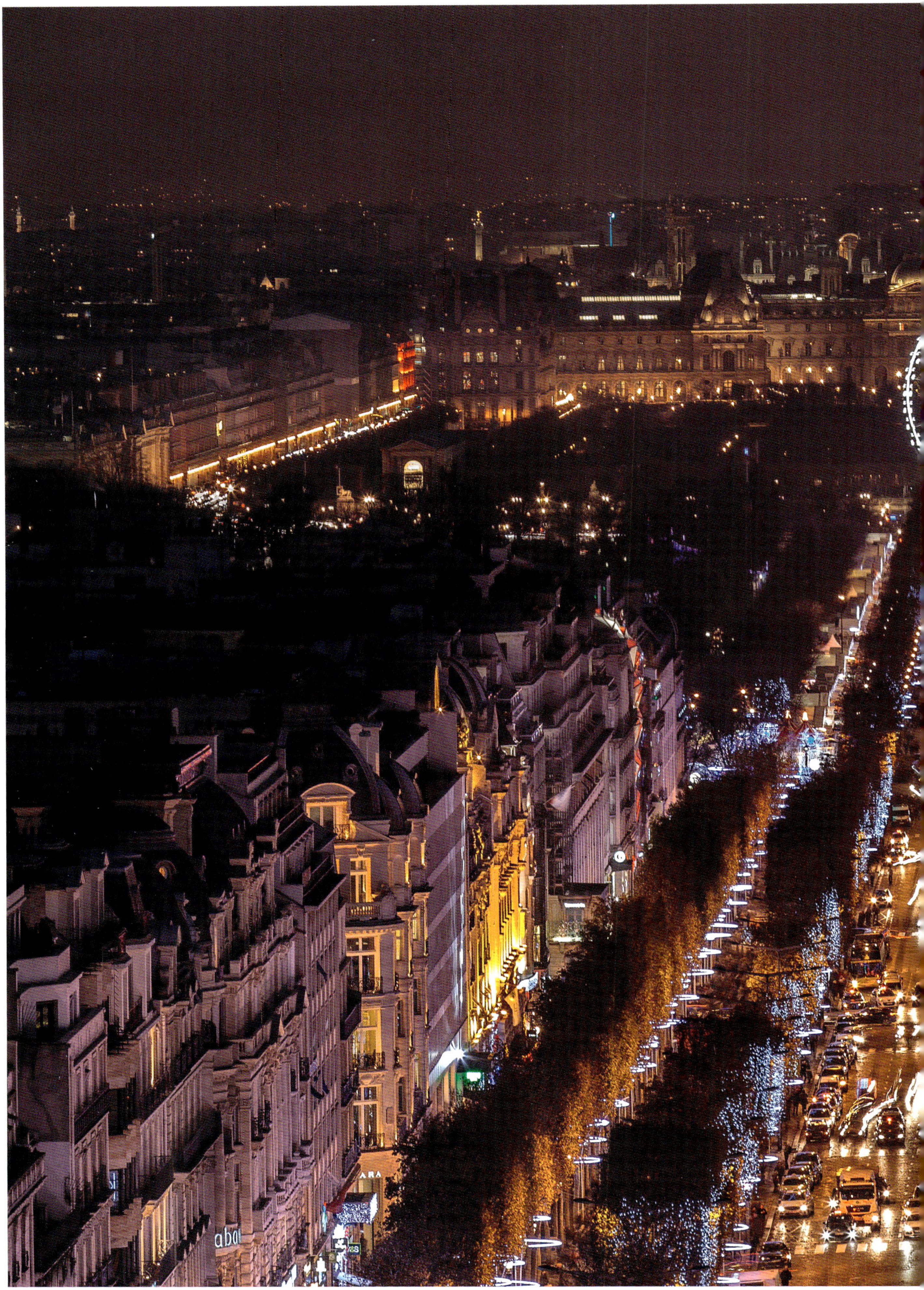

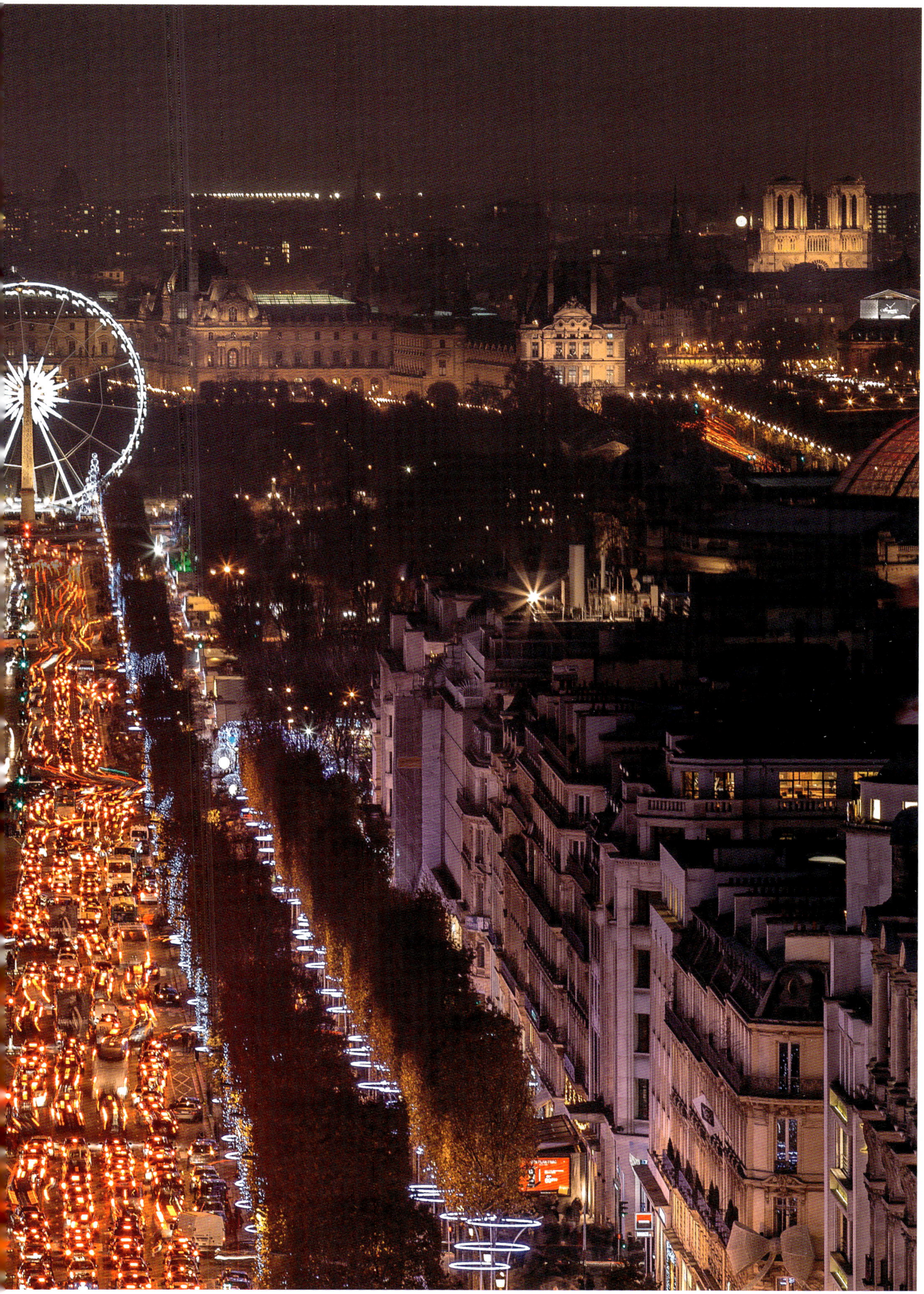

La Défense

PUTEAUX, COURBEVOIE, NANTERRE, LA GARENNE-COLOMBES (HAUTS-DE-SEINE)

Purpose-built at the beginning of the 1960s, the neighborhood houses the offices and headquarters of large companies that the capital, for lack of space, was having difficulty accommodating. At the end of the vast esplanade stands the Grande Arche, which since 1989 has offered an echo of the Arc de Carrousel and the Arc de Triomphe in Paris, all along the same axis.

The Thumb, by César.

The towers of La Défense and the Grande Arche.

On the square, the Quatre-Temps shopping center.

The CNIT (Center for New Industries and Technologies), the first building constructed in La Défense, in 1958.

The interior of the Palais de Tokyo.

Palais de Tokyo and the Musée d'Art Moderne
11 AND 13 AVENUE DU PRÉSIDENT-WILSON (16th)

Built for the World's Fair of 1937, the "Palais des Musées d'Art Moderne" mixes an elegant Art Deco decor and an ancient architectural vocabulary. Separated by a peristyle and terraces, a staircase overlooks the Seine, a museum in each wing. In the west wing is the site of contemporary creation, the Palais de Tokyo (named after the quay that it overlooks), and in the east wing, the Musée d'Art Moderne de la Ville de Paris. The first is a particularly active multidisciplinary space for all kinds of artist expression—painting, video, dance, sculpture, fashion—during diverse temporary events and exhibitions. The second houses the city's modern (from the early twentieth century until the 1960s) and contemporary (post-1960) collections. The biggest names of the twentieth century are represented: Matisse, Modigliani, Picasso, Bonnard, Foujita, Zadkine, Delaunay, as well as Tàpies, Basquiat, Penone, Buren, Raysse, di Rosa, Soulages, among many others.

The portico facing the Seine.

An aerial view of the Palais de Chaillot.  *The Eiffel Tower from the esplanade.*

Palais de Chaillot

1 PLACE DU TROCADÉRO-ET-DU-11-NOVEMBRE (16th)

The foyer of the Théâtre de Chaillot.  *The Gallery of Man at the Musée de l'Homme.*

It was built by Léon Azéma, Louis-Hippolyte Boileau and Jacques Carlu for the World's Fair of 1937. The architects very cleverly took advantage of the foundations of the old Palais du Trocadéro, itself used for the 1878 Fair, which included two small wings and a large central body flanked by two minarets. The idea was to recover the configuration of the curvilinear wings by dressing them in the monumental taste of the 1930s, and to replace the rotunda with an empty esplanade. No building was able to rival the Eiffel Tower opposite. It was much wiser to integrate it with the composition by making it a focal point. Glorifying peace and culture, on the building's four facade are quotes in gold lettering from Paul Valéry, including this one: "It depends on who passes / Whether I am tomb or treasure / Whether I speak or am mute / This is up to you / Friend, do not enter without desire."

The Gallery of Casts at the Cité de l'Architecture.

Musée Marmottan-Monet

2 RUE LOUIS-BOILLY (16th)

Camille on the Beach at Trouville, by Claude Monet, c. 1870–71.

The Bois de Boulogne's boats wait for visitors.

The facade facing the townhouse's garden.

Le Pont de l'Europe, Gare Saint-Lazare, by Claude Monet, 1877.

Before housing a museum, the building was a townhouse, occupied by art historian Paul Marmottan, a Napoleonic Empire specialist, who bequeathed his house and collections to the Académie des Beaux-Arts. The museum opened in 1934, presenting objects, paintings and furniture from the Napoleonic era gathered by Paul Marmottan and a group of primitive Italian and Flemish paintings collected by his father, Jules.

Because of the donations that followed, including from Michel Monet, son of the painter, and from the descendants of Berthe Morisot, the museum changed its focus, to become a Mecca of Impressionism. All the great names are represented: Renoir, Caillebotte, Jongkind, Degas, Manet, Pissarro, Sisley, Gauguin, and of course, Monet and Morisot. Marmottan has the honor of holding the world's largest collection of these works, with ninety-four paintings by Claude Monet and more than eighty works by Berthe Morisot.

Among other wonders, the museum houses the famous *Impression, Sunrise*, presented in 1874 in the rooms of the photographer, Nadar. This work sparked the name "Impressionism," when a journalist borrowed from its title to label the movement in order to mock it. But the quip quickly became a banner.

The Bois de Boulogne

16th ARRONDISSEMENT

These woods were built under the Second Empire for horse riding and carriage rides, or simply wandering. Artificial lakes were created, pathways designed, vegetation groomed and dotted with picturesque kiosks. The Pavilion de Bagatelle is an older inheritance, constructed by the Comte d'Artois, Louis XVI's brother in 1777, in just two months, as he had made a bet with his sister-in-law, Marie-Antoinette. In the nineteenth century, the property was transformed by the Marquis of Hertford, then by his son, Sir Richard Wallace, who built the Trianon.

The restaurant, Le Chalet des Îles.

The entrance to the metro station, Porte-Dauphine, designed by Hector Guimard.

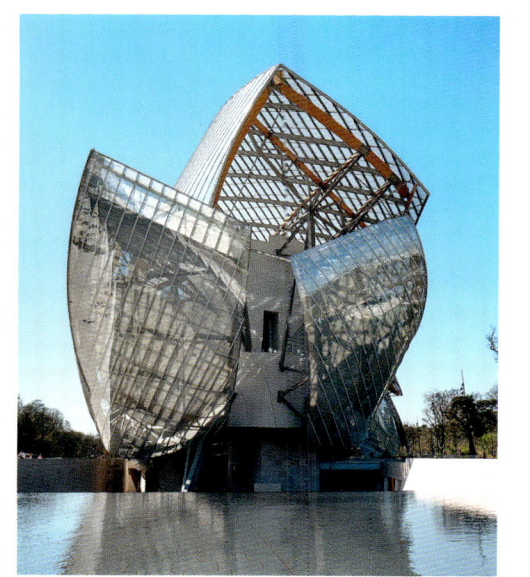

Fondation Louis-Vuitton

8 AVENUE DU MAHATMA-GANDHI (16th)

Since October 2014, the large sails of the spectacular vessel that is the Fondation Louis-Vuitton have been unfurled between the Jardin d'Acclimatation and the Bois de Boulogne. Architect Frank Gehry was inspired by the architecture of transparcy, from the Grand Palais to the Jardin d'Acclimatation's greenhouses, to create glass envelopes, structures housing contemporary art collections and exhibitions, as well as an auditorium.

Château de Versailles

PLACE D'ARMES (VERSAILLES, YVELINES)

Versailles was originally an aristocratic hunting lodge, before capturing the dreams of the young Louis XIV; the sovereign was only twenty-three when construction began. To supply the work, the king opened marble and stone quarries, created factories producing mirrors, silks, tapestries and porcelain. Forty thousand workers were mobilized, sometimes reinforced by the Sun King's troops in between military campaigns. Work on the château was driven by architect Louis Le Vau, while that of the garden was managed by André Le Nôtre. After Le Vau's death, Jules Hardouin-Mansart finalized the Hall of Mirrors and the chapel. The building work lasted almost fifty years, practically throughout the reign of Louis XIV, to achieve the "world's most beautiful château," a residence but also a political center and the Court's headquarters. These three aspects modeled very distinct spaces within the same container: the sovereigns' private sanctuaries seem almost modest compared to the official apartments reserved for the carrying out of protocol and ceremonies. And behind the gold, the château's backstage, sheltering all the machinery necessary for its administration, for the exercise of power and the maintenance of courtiership. Several hundred chambers and apartments are reserved for the latter.

A third of Versailles's building budget was devoted to transporting water to a site that was previously devoid of gardens, ponds and fountains. Aqueducts, canals and channels were built along dozens of kilometers to provide water for Versailles and amusements for the king and his court.

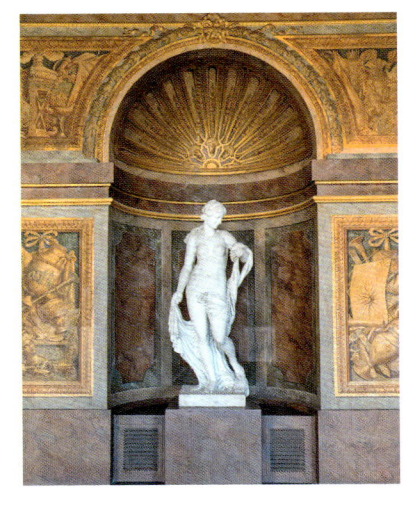

The facade facing the gardens.

Equestrian statue of Louis XIV.

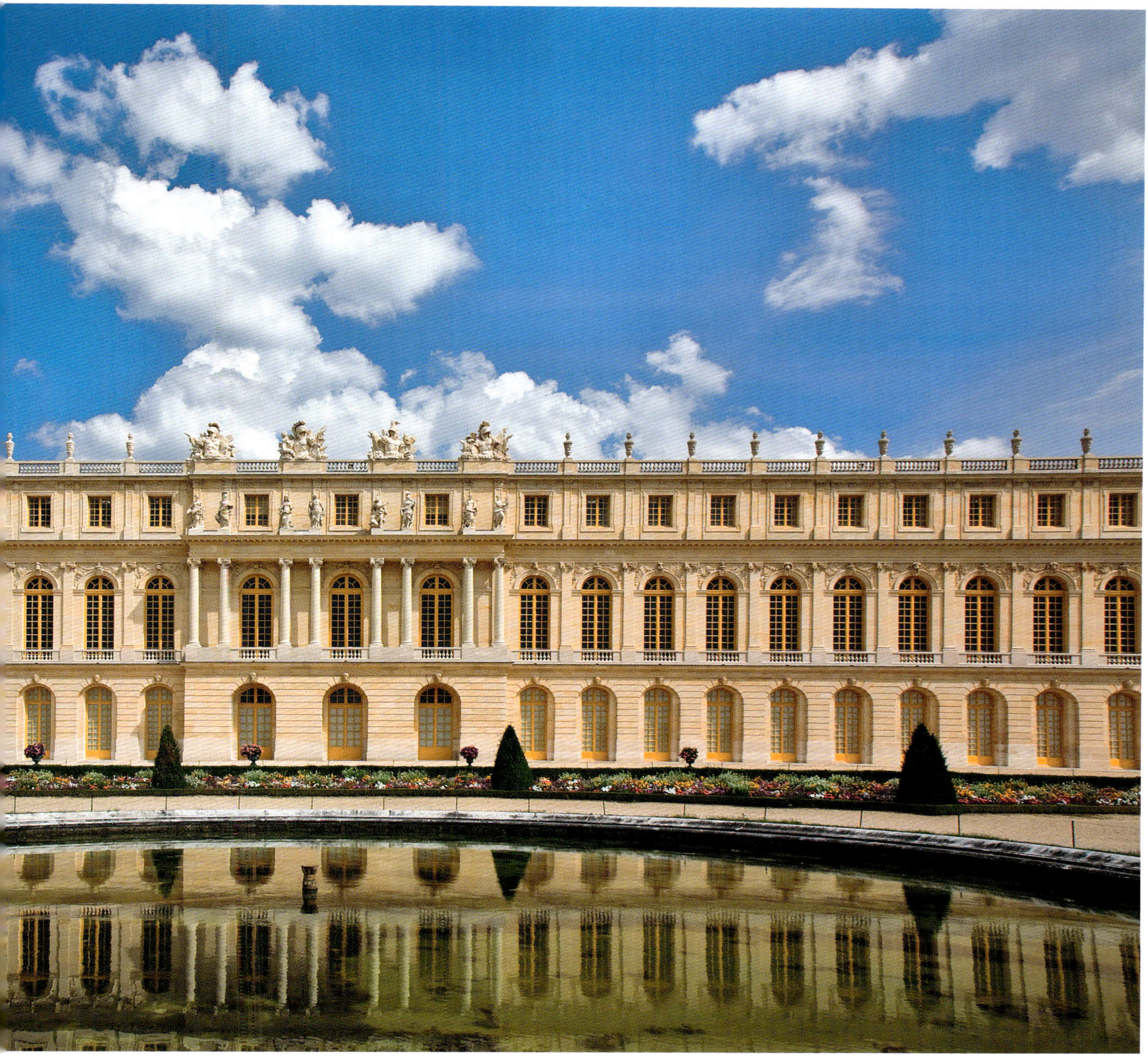

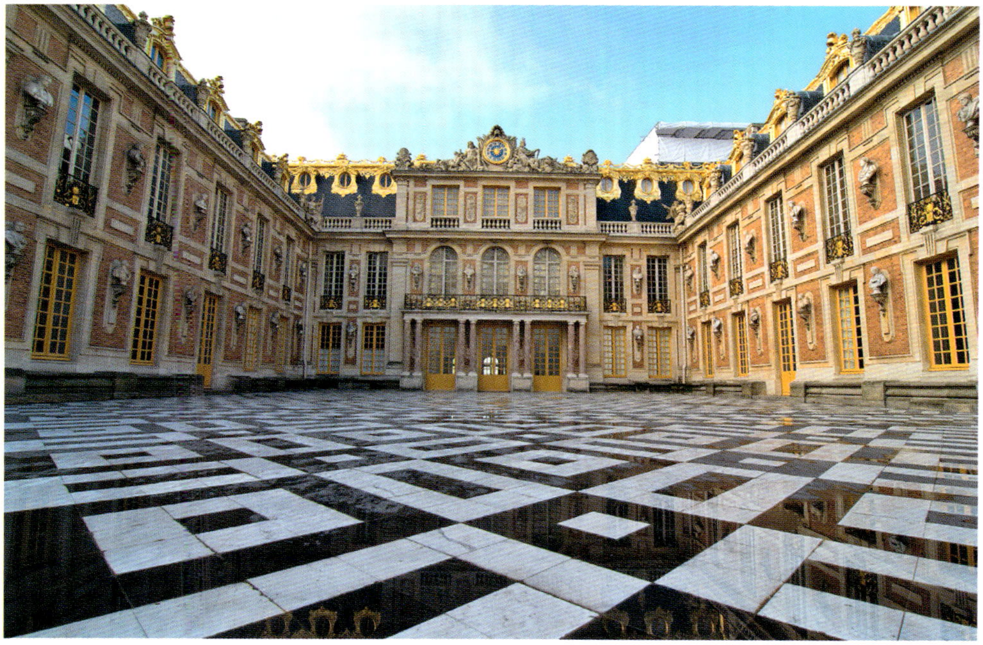

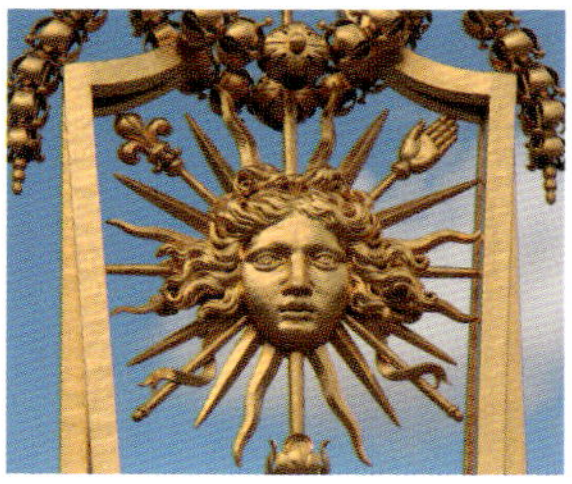

The Hall of Mirrors.

The Queen's Chamber.

The Royal Chapel.

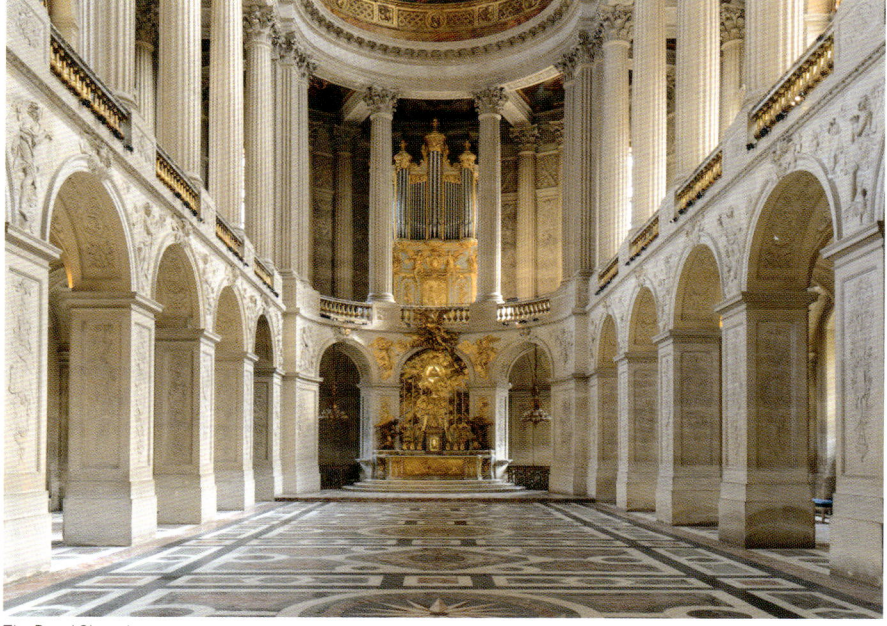

The Ceres Fountain, goddess of summer and the harvest.

Grotto of Tethys.

The Orangery.

The Latone Fountain.

A cottage in the queen's hamlet.

A factory on the Trianon estate.

The Marlborough tower in the queen's hamlet.

Temple of love, Petit Trianon.

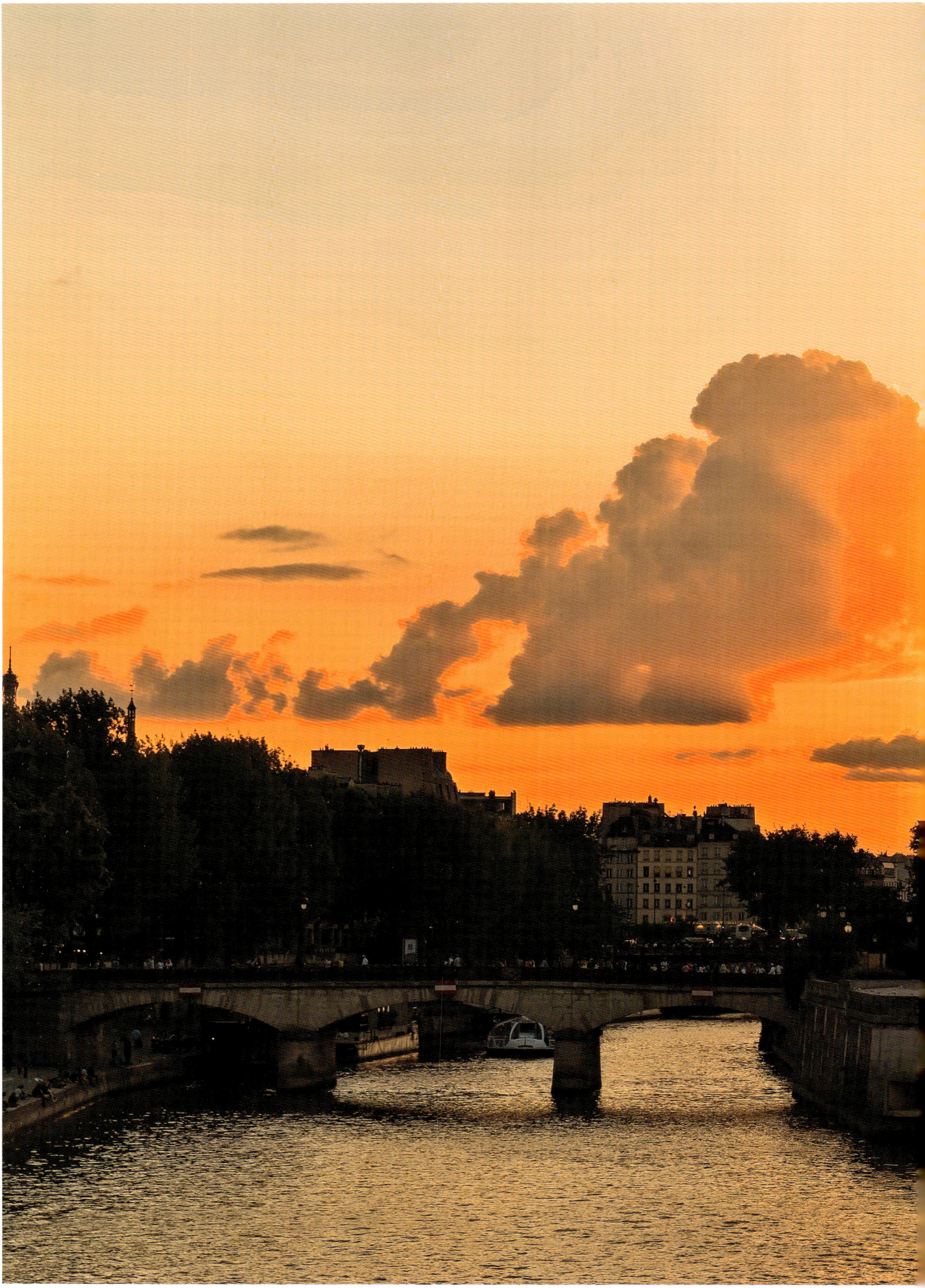

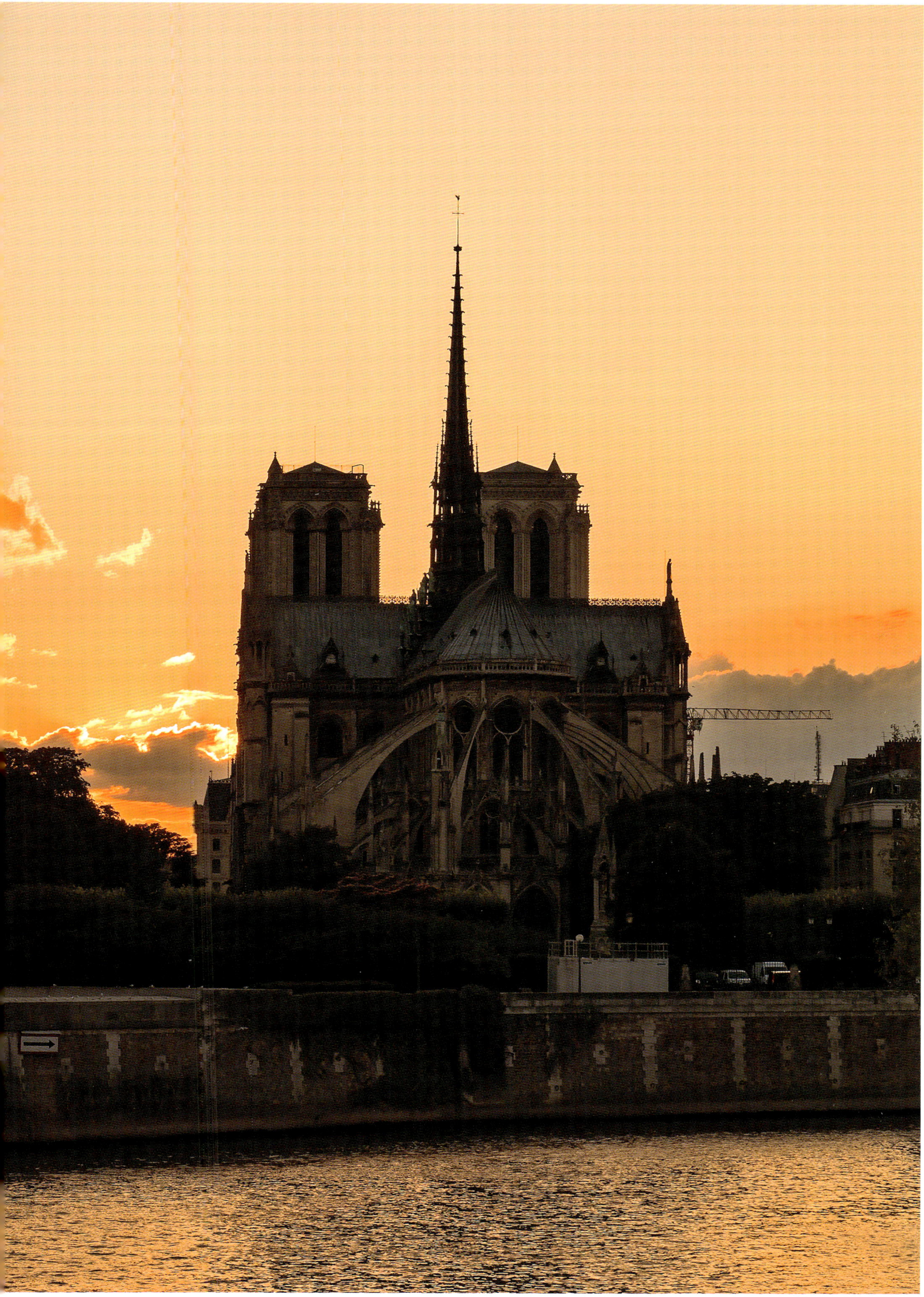

Editorial direction: François Besse
Editorial coordination: Mathilde Kressmann
Translation: Bronwyn Mahoney
Copy editing: Fui Lee Luk
Artistic direction: Isabelle Chemin
Images 3D: Tridimax, Paris

© Shutterstock and Wikimedia Commons

Printed in the European Union, April 2016
ISBN: 978-2-84096-977-8
Legal deposit: April 2016